What People Are ᵓ g About
Leᵔ

Devrah dissec   unravels the only permanent solu   we discover the many faces of guilt and   ..as undermined our lives. This book is a comforti   ιο anyone who has felt the pain of not being good enough   ..ιeved they did something wrong, but it is also a journey of discovering the spiritual solution to guilt that is our gateway to freedom.
Jonathan Parker, Ph.D. www.soulsolution.net

Brilliant! Absolutely Brilliant. It is so rare for there to be a book that simply shows what the deepest truth is regarding who we are, and the illusion of the world that we get trapped in. Devrah Laval has succeeded in creating a leading edge book that translates the process of awakening our consciousness in a way that we can all understand. I recommend this to anyone who is questioning who they are and the role that guilt plays in keeping us immobilized, both individually and collectively.
Anjali Hill, International Seminar Leader and Counselor

Leap to Freedom is an engaging and captivating look at the cycles of shame and guilt that define us as individuals, as communities and even as entire countries. Devrah Laval brings powerful insights into the realm of Oneness Consciousness, as it relates to guilt. She brings heart and compassion to the science behind this illusion of reality, and gives both seasoned and novice seekers an entirely new perspective on the role of guilt in shaping our lives. *Leap to Freedom* is poignant, powerful and cohesive. Unlike any other book I've ever read, it synthesizes wisdom from both Eastern and Western traditions to present one whole irrefutable reality, wherein we are not guilty and never have been.
S. Young, Interior Designer, Seattle, Washington

Devrah Laval's *Leap to Freedom* takes guilt and turns it inside out and upside down – and all for the better. With profound insight and honesty, Devrah deftly weaves a new tale for the age-old story on guilt. Shaped by Devrah's own experiences, innate knowledge and profound understanding, *Leap to Freedom* guides readers to new perspectives. Using historical, spiritual and scientific references, Devrah allows readers to understand, distil, and transform this thing called guilt. Once the new story on guilt settles in, readers can disown any guilt they had presumed was their own.

Dee Willock, author of *Falling into Easy: Help For Those Who Can't Meditate*

Leap to Freedom offers gorgeous wisdom and simple tools that assist in transcending the complex and screwball beliefs currently messing with our authentic self. Devrah recounts personal experiences to exemplify dark modes of thinking and magically turns a mood into a lighthouse, guiding us toward clear thinking and profound grace. Guilt, when examined under the microscope of Devrah's investigation is seen for what it is: a mournful and inappropriate nagging waste of time. *Leap to Freedom* is one of the strangest reads I've ever had: painfully funny, but at times sad and frightening. While inside the pages, I became aware of how pervasive is guilt's mischief. Devrah's fortunate readers will need a little courage in order to activate the tools, but with the help of quotes from our ancient masters and Devrah's ability to present her modern day knowledge, you'll soon discover *Leap to Freedom* is a beautiful, accessible read, and ultimately a celebration of life.

Glynis Davies is an actor/writer living in Vancouver.

Devrah Laval's book *Leap to Freedom* is a groundbreaking treatise on radical awakening and personal freedom. She has seamlessly woven together science, mysticism and yogic thought in a way that springs the door open for all of us to grasp the truth of unconditional love. For centuries mankind has been caught in a web of suffering and victimization – an unconscious dream state of illusion – sometimes called the matrix. Devrah offers profound insights from her own mystic's journey on how guilt has kept us caught in this perceived separation from our infinite source. This book is a must for anyone on a true path of ultimate awakening.

Karen Rae Wilson, Singer, Social Activist and Spiritual Visionary
www.wisdomculture.com

Leap to Freedom

Healing Quantum Guilt

Leap to Freedom

Freedom

Healing Quantum Guilt

Devrah Laval

BOOKS

Winchester, UK
Washington, USA

First published by O-Books, 2013
O-Books is an imprint of John Hunt Publishing Ltd., Laurel House, Station Approach,
Alresford, Hants, SO24 9JH, UK
office1@jhpbooks.net
www.johnhuntpublishing.com

For distributor details and how to order please visit the 'Ordering' section on our website.

Text copyright: Devrah Laval 2012

ISBN: 978 1 78099 567 0

A CIP catalogue record for this book is available from the British Library.

Design: Stuart Davies

Printed and bound by CPI Group (UK) Ltd, Croydon, CR0 4YY

We operate a distinctive and ethical publishing philosophy in all
areas of our business, from our global network of authors to
production and worldwide distribution.

CONTENTS

To all of my great teachers who draw from the same immaculate source and especially to my greatest teacher, my mom.

Acknowledgements

To everyone who assisted with putting this book together, especially JP Stevan, Dee Willock, Glynis Davies, S. Young, Anjali Hill, Michele Guest, Julius Kiskis, and Dr. Anne McMurtry.

Introduction

Whether we are rich or poor, religious, agnostic, or atheist, we all suffer because of our unconscious belief in sin and guilt, both of which lie at the core of all our decisions and actions. But what if everything we've been taught about sin, and the need to feel guilt, has been a lie? What if sin is the result of forgetting who we are and where we've come from? And what if we don't actually make decisions to act? But rather life unfolds; actions "happen" and then our thought about it comes *after* the fact. Sound bizarre? Welcome to the world of Quantum thought.

The purpose of this book is to offer a way out from these limited and debilitating beliefs that we've blindly accepted, by exploring how and why sin and guilt are illusions. What if we no longer have to live in fear of suffering and eternal damnation, or be plagued by constant nagging doubt or unworthiness brought on by the beliefs in sin and guilt? What if, instead, we could live every moment in the state of love and peace, and thereby be better able to fulfill our true purpose?

Leap to Freedom will change your perception of guilt forever by freeing you from the beliefs that you are guilty, sinful, and unworthy. *Leap to Freedom* will help you identify with your true self and with your inherent oneness with all beings. You will learn to empower yourself and others in positive loving ways rather than in combative ways. With support from scientific discoveries as well as ancient spiritual teachings, you will be able to dispel the belief that you are the "doer" of action.

You will better understand how and why we have so many difficulties in our lives. Instead, you will realize that taking responsibility for a new way of thinking is all that is required for you to transform your experiences from pain and victimization to peace and freedom. This then leads to a new perspective on your relationships with which you can ultimately end the conflicts both within yourself and with others. Take the leap and discover your own freedom and interconnectedness with all beings and from this point offer the highest service to mankind.

We will start off by questioning old conditionings and beliefs about sin and guilt, in order to understand how and why we are stuck in an endless wheel of karma brought about solely in the belief in doership-actions that originate from ego. We will explore contemplations and exercises that will help us to experience and ultimately live this new paradigm – that everything we've taken to be true and real is actually an illusion. We will empower ourselves with not only the truth intellectually but also with a deeper truth that will allow for experiential wisdom, which makes our truth our own.

Foreword

What prompted Devrah Laval to write this book was the same impulse that prompted the young Buddha to leave the comfort of his father's palace and seek out and investigate the causes of suffering. In this case, Devrah explores the causes of suffering that are behind unconscious guilt, which is due to the mistaken belief that we have separated from Source.

Devrah experienced the widespread influence of unconscious guilt not only in herself but also in her clients, friends and family. Because of her limitless compassion, she made a solemn resolution to go to the very root of this problem, to examine it from every angle and to provide some much needed medicine that could reverse it.

Devrah's courage demanded that she birth the solution from within her own experience. Devrah knew that only when she got to the root of this in her own life, could she speak with any authority and thereby assist others. The precious nectar of freedom, extracted from this search, is passed onto every soul who joins her on this journey. While researching this book, she searched for a solution for why this widespread unconscious guilt lives in all of us. In this very comprehensive study of unconscious guilt, Devrah points out that the root of guilt is the misperception that we have separated from Source.

The Buddha went so far as to say that the misbelief that we are separate from one another and from the very fabric of the universe is what causes us to suffer, (His Anatma-Vada doctrine). Therefore our shame, guilt, low self-esteem and our tendency to mistrust and attack each other all stem from this belief in separation.

The good news, reported by all enlightened beings and saints, is that none of us have ever been truly separated from Divine Source. To quote the great Hindu saint, Shankaracharya, *"The only obstacle to emancipation is ignorance and there is no other hindrance; for emancipation is eternal and identical to the Self."* Similarly the Hindu saint Ramana Maharshi said, *"Our real nature is liberation but we imagine that we are bound ... we make strenuous efforts to become free although all the while we are free."*

The process of being delivered from unconscious guilt and the misbelief in separation is like waking up from a dream. Thus, Devrah's book, *Leap to Freedom,* ushers in a major paradigm shift, inverting our sense of reality.

This can be compared to the dream of the Taoist sage, Chuang-tsu who said: *"I do not know whether I was then a man dreaming I was a butterfly, or whether I am now a butterfly dreaming I am a man."*

We need to be reminded of this perennial paradox again and again, for we so easily forget that we are all woven out of the one Divine Fabric. The Chandogya Upanishad, a sacred Hindu text describes this paradoxical realization as follows: Tat Tvam Asi, translated as That Thou Art, in other words, we are already One.

But the most unexpected and definitive validation of this state of unity and oneness comes from the realm of science. Devrah cites numerous scientific examples from quantum physics that support the idea of oneness, and not unlike Einstein's Unified Field Theory, to merge or unify science with spirituality. Devrah also states that we cannot trust our perceptions of this world based solely on our senses alone but by taking a quantum leap to freedom, we can finally let go of the heavy weight of unconscious guilt and shame.

Thank you Devrah for taking us on this sacred journey and holding all of our hearts in your immense heart. I know you would say in response that there is really only One Divine Heart, wherein we all dwell.

Shirley Anne McMurtry Ph. D. Comparative Religions

PART I

QUANTUM GUILT –

THE FINAL ILLUSION

From the One Light, the entire universe welled up. So who is good and who is bad?

Kabir

QUANTUM GUILT

In the beginning there was nothing. No world, no life, no time, no space – and no consciousness. Then, according to the standard Big Bang theory, out of nowhere came an infinitesimally small, infinitely hot and infinitely dense, "something", called a singularity, which expanded outward with a tremendous amount of energy.

All of time was contained within this single instant. And this instant began, and ended, simultaneously. This expansion has been called a supernatural event, that is, one outside of the natural realm. This took place approximately fourteen billion years ago.

"In this instant, all physical laws and the fate of every molecule was pre-determined. Everything that would seemingly occur was already set in motion in that instant, and in fact could not occur any other way." (1)

Hence, all of existence is scripted and has already happened but is being played out within the illusion of time. Like a star that has died, we can still see its light thousands of years later, likewise with an echo, which reverberates long after we have come and gone. This realm, that we think is reality, is also an illusion. It has already come and gone and we are mere shadows of what occurred in that instant.

We're almost fourteen billion years old, give or take a few millennia. From the echo of one instantaneous event, the One became the many and universes were projected outward from nothingness. Notions of time and space were created so as to hold all that came afterward, including the idea of physicality and separation. The initial singularity was so immeasurably small, it could be called quantum. From this infinitesimally small, dense singularity, were also born fear and guilt, which are the thickest veils, between illusion and reality. They were born out of the belief that we are separate from our source. Quantum guilt originated and arose as a by-product, or a child, of this separation.

Along with the expansion of this universe, guilt has expanded to become the biggest problem we all face. Guilt keeps the illusion of separation alive by making us forget our source and our innocence. The moment that consciousness saw a separate 'other' we experienced fear and felt we had done something wrong. Thus we began to chase the multiple forms that exist in our world, believing them to be concrete and permanent and hoping that they would somehow return us to our oneness. By searching duality to reclaim oneness, we have made the material world real, reinforcing our belief in separation.

The Big Bang can be seen to overlap with other origin stories, such as Creationism. If one believes that God orchestrated this whole creation in the first place, (the biblical description of the seven days of creation being a simple way to explain what had taken approximately fourteen billion years to unfold), then both the Big Bang and the Creationism stories are equally valid – while at the same time being equally untrue – as they both only exist within the dream.

However, for the sake of discussion, we'll explore this "reality" as if our beliefs and concepts about it are indeed true.

Science cannot say where the singularity came from or where it existed prior to space and time. It's as though this singularity just "appeared." The Hebrew Torah refers to the first day of Creation as, "the day of Oneness." Over time, the "Oneness" began to evolve into "the many." If God the Creator, "The One" used this singularity to create "The Many" then we are still one with "God", still perfect and innocent. We are told that something separated from, or out of nothing, (some consider the nothing to be God), at the moment of creation. However, just as a dream seems to have its own separate existence, so too this world we call reality is just a play of consciousness that one day we will awaken from.

Expansion occurred out of this 'Oneness' and from its splintering came sound, light, space and time, as well as galaxies, worlds, and creatures big and small, including us. The story of the Garden of Eden is a wonderful metaphor for the split that occurred when Adam and Eve acted on Satan's advice, "To eat an apple from the tree of the knowledge of good and evil." Satan represents the lie and the belief that we are capable of separating from our Source. The Tree of Knowledge represents duality and separation.

There is yet another possibility that offers a quantum leap in perceiving reality.

Physicist David Bohm has interpreted physicist Alain Aspect's findings, by positing that this universe is a superhologram in which the past, present and future all exist simultaneously. Bohm believed that Alain Aspect's findings imply that, *"Objective reality does not exist, that despite its apparent solidity the universe is at heart a phantasm, a gigantic and splendidly detailed hologram."* (2) Michael Talbot describes this superhologram as the, "Matrix that has given birth to everything in our universe, at the very least it contains every subatomic particle that has been or will be – every configuration of matter and energy that is possible, from snowflakes to quasars … a sort of cosmic storehouse of 'All That Is.'" (3)

The Hindu's refer to this separation/expansion as a world of multiplicity. However, just as in a hologram wherein the whole is contained in all of the parts, so do we each, though seemingly different and separate, contain the whole/Divine within ourselves. Our purpose in life is to choose the truth over the illusion.

Kahlil Gibran wrote, *"It's not that God is in my heart but rather that I am in the heart of God."*

Fast forward to today…

Problems cannot be solved at the same level of thinking that created them. Albert Einstein

So in our fast paced world, what would it look like to choose the truth over the illusion? The problem is that we can't tell the difference, as the illusion seems to be the truth to us. Unfortunately, all of our choices seem to be limited to what we can perceive or conceive, but these are based on the externals that are part of the illusion, or projections that we place on what we see in our world. As a result of responding to life from illusion/ego as opposed to from a higher vision, we suffer. For example, we know how difficult it is to resolve a recurring relationship problem and we do our best to fix uncomfortable life situations. We might leave a marriage only to arrive at a new relationship with the same unmet needs. We find a new job, move to a different country only to discover we are still on the same planet and nothing has really changed. No matter how much we try to change anything in this world, it is like moving the furniture around from one end of the room to the other. The problem is we are still in the room with the same furniture. It looks different but really isn't. Our problems cannot be resolved at our present level of knowledge because we believe the dream, as being true and real. We need to take a quantum leap and make a dramatic advance in our understanding of what is at the root of our suffering-conflict, fear and guilt.

The enemy that we know is not the threat, but rather the enemy that we are unconscious of, is what creates all of our problems.

You may have heard of the adage, "Love makes the world go around," but in truth it's unconscious guilt that, "makes the world go around."

Becoming aware of this unconscious guilt can dramatically affect a person's whole life. We don't recognize it as guilt because it feels more like a very deep upset or fear. Yet guilt permeates everything in our world and has kept us separate from others and the Divine. As we learn how to correct our projections and misperceptions, we can begin to reclaim our power, align with our true worth and discover our purpose in life thereby dissolving the guilt that binds us.

These truths will implant within you an understanding that no one will ever be able to take from you. They will turn your world inside out. You will never have the same relationship with sin and guilt and the idea of doer-ship again for you will always remember that we are all one substance and life is already scripted and will unfold as it will.

Do not open this book unless you want to take a quantum leap to freedom, to a whole new level of understanding. We are dealing with the real issue, the core guilt that we don't even know we have. All of our conflicts are simply symptoms of this quantum guilt. No matter how large or small our problems might feel, they all come from this one core guilt – the belief that we've actually separated from our very source. The good news? Separation is a lie. We are not separate from our Source, and we have the power to dispel this wrong belief and begin to change our world by healing quantum guilt and transforming it into quantum love.

Because everything is constantly being diluted by nothing, we can experience it as everything. (4) Tor Norretranders

1.1 THE END OF GUILT

When we no longer believe in guilt, the world, as we know it will end. A new world will arise, a world without doubt, fear, unworthiness and pride. A world founded on love, forgiveness, compassion and oneness. We will remember who we are, we will remember what we have forgotten, and we will know where we belong.

In a dream, I was play wrestling with a friend by a pool of water. We were both wearing big boots and battle fatigues. I could not see a face, but I could feel how much I cared for this person. As we continued, our wrestling became more intense and I vividly recall accidentally kicking my friend with my heavy boot, which unbalanced him and caused him to fall into a deep pool of dark water. I remember the shock. I had no intention of harming him. I desperately tried to save him, but his body felt like a dead weight.

I was worried that the kick might have knocked him out. I called for help, but no one was around. I struggled for what seemed like an eternity until finally I managed to retrieve his body, only to discover that he was dead. In a panic, I dragged the body to a treed area and dug him a shallow grave. I felt I needed to hide what had happened because I somehow knew that no one would understand that my actions were innocent – without malicious intent.

The next morning, I awoke from the dream in deep shock. As I looked around the room, I barely recognized the surroundings – as though I was still in the dream. It was as if time had dissolved and no boundaries existed between the present and past. I did not know what was the dream and what was reality anymore because I felt that I was traversing through unknown territory. Terrified and confused, I began grasping pieces of furniture and objects in the room, I recall even grabbing hold of the rim of the bathroom sink just to see if it was solid and real –

fully expecting the sink to completely dissolve in my hand. I tried with all my might to ground myself in the midst of this transcendental experience. The veil that separated the dream world from the waking state had evaporated and left me feeling like Alice in Wonderland. As I tried to go about my day, I kept asking myself, "Whom did I kill?" I traced back through my whole life from the time I was a young child to recall if I had actually harmed someone. I was grief-stricken, and I was unable to function normally, so I just cancelled my day. Exhausted, I sat down on the floor, leaned against a wall, and prayed, "Please forgive me, please show me what I did."

I felt as though I had committed the ultimate Sin, and I no longer could distinguish between my sleeping dream and my so-called waking life. I'd heard about this sort of transcendent experience, wherein the boundaries of space and time dissolve, and because it came so unexpectedly, I had no understanding of how to deal with it. Feeling helpless, I closed my eyes and started meditating, hoping to get some insight. Then, after a long while, something began to change in my conscious awareness. I was no longer in an uneventful meditation; instead, I was catapulted into a greatly expanded perspective. I felt like my whole skull was being pulled and stretched upward and I had no control over any of the events that were unfolding. Then I found myself at the very top of a mountain sitting with a being, a deep love / a God-like presence that was giving me a true vision of what was real. I now witnessed my "bad" dream, from a higher level of consciousness – higher than I had viewed anything before.

Simultaneously, I also experienced the most love I'd ever felt in my whole life. Although I was alone, the feeling of love was so thick; it felt as if a thousand angels surrounded me. What was unique was that I had a different point of reference. I wasn't limited to my physical body. On the contrary I was in no way different from anything around me; I was made of the same substance.

Being one with this divine presence, I reviewed this "bad" dream once again but as a detached observer. It was shown to me in an odd way: as I watched what appeared to be below me, I recall looking upon my own confused self with the utmost compassion and love, rather than the guilt and fear that I had felt when I had experienced the dream the first time. What had the greatest impact on me was that I was shown how absolutely pure and innocent I really was, contrary to a belief I had always carried that I was guilty and somehow inherently bad. I was awestruck at the recognition of my inherent purity. This sin that I thought I had committed was shown to be just a bad dream, not unlike watching a movie. As I kept viewing the images from the dream, I saw that the *entire world,* believed to be real, was no different – it too, was just a dream. I awoke from my night time dream, believing it to be true and real, only to enter into a daytime dream actually believing that I was awake when in fact this world that I thought to be 'reality,' was yet another dream.

In this awake dream, I was watching a movie of my life, with a myriad of characters coming and going in meaningless movements that to them were serious and real. It was like observing a made-up child's game, similar to cowboys and Indians, where the characters just keep on fighting and knocking one another down, but then get up again and move on to the next scene. I felt I was waking up from the dream I had thought was my life, and I was actually standing outside of my life. In that moment, I realized that the person I thought I was didn't exist. The person in the dream I had identified with was just a scripted character. Who I truly am is something far greater and all encompassing. This moment changed my reality and turned it upside down. I saw just how much time and energy had been wasted living in conflict and trying so hard to be perfect when all I needed to do was to rest in the deep, wordless place, which needed no script.

As I sat in this exalted place, I realized that nothing was real but this profound love. No judgment, no blame, no guilt of any kind existed. Only Oneness – only love. This is where I/we truly live. Everything else is illusion based on strange beliefs in separation and guilt. All such notions are relevant only within the scripted dream but have no place outside of it. In fact, I understood that we are loved unconditionally, and that guilt and sin do not even exist.

I realized that the rules of our illusory world are very different from what is real, spirit. The truth as I experienced it is that we are loved beyond our limited forms more than we can possibly imagine – we are with this Divine source always. In fact, we've never left, contrary to what our illusion would have us believe: the physical world is like a dream; and just like in a dream, we do not "do" anything, we are puppets being played. Just as a dream is illusory, our so-called "reality" is also a dream and therefore, guilt is unreal, as it can only exist within the illusion. The moment I truly understood this, deep shivers conveyed, "You are forgiven," and reverberated throughout my whole being. I felt as if every sin I thought I had committed was cleansed. As this was happening, I knew that I didn't really need forgiveness; I saw absolutely that there really is nothing to forgive because we are loved unconditionally beyond anything we could possibly conceive of in this world. The cleansing I experienced felt like an infusion of love, bathing in itself and playing with the concept of forgiveness.

I saw that at the level of Truth, which is where we truly exist – there is no separation. We are all made of the same substance and hence already one. There is only One, only Love. Love is all that is real.

Nothing real can be threatened.
Nothing unreal exists.
Herein lies the peace of God.
A Course In Miracles (5)

1.2 THE AFTERMATH

After such a profound experience, I needed some time to integrate it and to become more grounded in everyday life. I felt as though I was living in two worlds, but now I knew what the real world was. I better understood what it meant to be, "Living in this world but not of it."

At first I felt quite euphoric, even ecstatic at times, as I felt the words, "You are forgiven," continually resound in my heart as waves upon waves. I felt as pure and innocent as a child. The divine presence that I was a part of bathed me in a magnificent love, and I wanted to share this love with everyone. I felt free and not bound by this world, which I saw as a game, an illusion.

My relationships took on a different quality. I stopped looking at others' shortcomings, limitations, and perceived sins, and I could actually see the great love and perfection that lay beneath their exterior personality and ego. I knew that at the highest level, we are all forgiven from the illusion of sin because we are already one with Divinity.

Over time, the experience paled and I became more "normal." But what remains is the knowledge that everyone I meet is actually my own self, reflected back to me, because we are all just one being. Each one of us is love, and every loving or forgiving thought that we have reverberates and uplifts the entire world. Similarly, every unloving thought equally affects our world by creating pain. The latter happens only because we forget who we are, and we slide into the darkness of the illusion of separation, pain, guilt, fear, sin, and blame, to mention only a few. The key is taking responsibility for everything that we perceive in our world as being an extension of us. Even though our character is scripted, as long as we are here, it makes sense that we would want to bring love and compassion to all of the challenging people and situations we encounter. Especially as we are, in effect, only dealing with ourselves.

A dear friend of mine related an experience that he had with one of his teachers who was trying to get him to understand what projection was. One day he was expressing anger and frustration at some perceived injustice and his teacher pulled out a small mirror and held it up in front of his face. This enraged him even more and his anger grew to a climax as he felt an incredible aloneness because all he saw was his own reflection. He collapsed in tears because his experience showed him that there was no one 'out there' to be angry with and that's when he realized that when he got angry with another, it was only himself that he was hurting – we are all made of the same substance. So in this dream that we are all having, the noblest thing that we can do is to bring our light and love to all of the illusions we encounter, thereby dispelling our belief in separation and guilt.

One of the biggest realizations I had was that guilt is our last illusion. From this dream I began to understand that this guilt game we play is the ultimate separator between us and our source. It acts like a wedge between our selves and our oneness with the Divine. Guilt's power is so great because we believe that it protects us from making wrong actions. But really, guilt's only service is to infuse us with fear and negative feelings about others and ourselves. Guilt hides where we can't easily find it, hiding in every situation and person in our life. In this way we are reminded that we have done something wrong and are led to believe that we're not good enough to be the love – the love we already are.

Just as guilt is an illusion, this world is a dream, a fantasy. It is an invention of the mind, based on separation and incorrect understanding. We believe that we have separated from God and as a result "He" is punishing us and so we in turn punish ourselves as well as others, hence, wars and conflicts of every kind persist. This is the illusion, the lie – the dream. This is not unlike when children, who are seen as perfect and sinless by their parents, go out to play and create an imaginary world filled with enemies and bad guys who need to be punished or vanquished for their "sins." Then, once the illusory game is over, they return home to resume their place as guiltless and perfectly loved children.

Similarly, where there is no guilt, there is no need for punishment. We are loved unconditionally in the same way as the children. The problem is we believe the rules of this game we play to be true. We are required to buy into the belief that we are sinners, guilty and deserving of punishment. Our world and the people in it reflect this belief everyday. We believe that we are separate from others, which leads to our belief that others are impediments to our sense of peace. This sense of peace comes only when we know that we are all one. As the Bible says, "Do unto others as you would have them do unto you." We have never been separated from Source, although the world's religions would have us believe on a mass scale that we are guilty. Why else would babies need to be baptized even before they can speak? Basically they are deemed to be born impure and needing to be baptized into a world filled with duality, good/bad – right/wrong etc. Then, structures are created in order to justify this duality/separation from Source, such as the eastern concept of Karma.

According to Eastern teachings, Karma rules this realm, that is, as a law of action and reaction, cause and effect and its ensuing outcomes, experienced as reward or punishment. As a result, we feel trapped by guilt because we feel a deep and terrible responsibility for believing that we've separated from others, our Source and ourselves. This guilt is insidious, much like an implant that we aren't even aware of; it's been so ingrained in us that we punish ourselves for it unconsciously all of the time. It serves to keep us trapped in an illusion of pain and suffering. Guilt is the glue that binds this scripted dream that we're in. If you look deeply, you will see that guilt underlies everything in our life. Only when we step out of the dream, do we begin to feel relief from our bondage.

Guilt is an illusion that we mistake for "reality" which only appears when we believe we are the body alone. Yet, there's help. Many saints have come forth to teach us the following:

"God's love is there for all, no matter what we have done. Unconditional love accepts everyone."
Sant Rajinder Singh

The Persian Mystic, Hafiz advises the only way out of this dilemma of duality is to ...

" ... Become free, become free from this whole world like Hafiz."

1.3 THE SPLIT

The universe began when nothing saw itself in the mirror.
Tor Norretranders

Every path has an explanation, based on its cultural and spiritual understandings of what transpired at the beginning of time/creation. Even science has its beliefs that continue to evolve, with the most familiar one being "The Big Bang."

In an article on the website: *All About Science*, (6) Houdmann et al. say that three astrophysicists, Steven Hawking, George Ellis, and Roger Penrose focused their attention on Einstein's Theory of Relativity and its implications regarding the notions of time. Their calculations showed that time and space had a finite beginning, which corresponded to the origin of matter and energy – the Big Bang. Prior to this, nothing existed, neither space, nor time, nor matter, nor energy – nothing.

Just as each religion or path has some variation on the creation story, they all generally seem to acknowledge sin, guilt and separation from Source. As a result, we have created baptisms and Mikvah Baths and many purification processes in various spiritual traditions, as symbolic gestures to cleanse ourselves of the sin that resulted from this original separation.

The purpose of these various forms of purification is to make us "worthy" to experience a God or to receive blessings of a particular god. However, the real purpose for these cleansing rituals is to remove the veils that keep us blinded to the truth and to help us realize that we never needed the purification in the first place because we already are one and have never been apart from our Source and could therefore never be unworthy of love. Anybody who experiences the absolute truth of who they are discovers that there's never been any such separation and can see this guilt-free world as it is – a dream or a play where we are merely the actors.

Many paths and religions use the belief in separation to anthropomorphize Source by turning it into a male god with human attitudes and characteristics, someone who can love us and at the same time judge us, which leaves us bereft, in pain and longing. This "humanized" god supposedly tells us that we will never be able to reach the goal of re-uniting with "Him" unless we do it right, whatever "right" is. So religions create lofty ideals for us to strive to live our lives by, which only perpetuate the guilt cycle and the feeling of futility, whenever we fail in our thoughts, words or actions. Attaining a saintly life is almost impossible while in the human form for the average person. No wonder we are frustrated and angry because the god we have trusted does not seem to love us unconditionally, or so it appears.

According to the bible, Adam chose to go against God and hence, separated from "Him". We too believe that we, somewhere and somehow, have chosen to leave our source, God, and are carrying guilt for abandoning "Him", not unlike a child who runs away, (or moves away) from home believing that they are now free from the parents. But regardless of the age of the child, the bond with the parents cannot be broken by mere distance for both the child and his parents are of the same essence. We are all made of the same substance and are one with Source. Imagine God, separating from Itself and having that separate part believe that it could somehow be bad or sinful. Only in a dream could this happen. This life, this reality is all taking place in a dream, and just as events in a dream seem real while you are asleep, this dream (that we call reality) can only exist while we are spiritually asleep.

Every action of cruelty or separation involves treating another as an object outside oneself. Dualism is said to be behind all sin. Just as a wave in the ocean cannot be separate from the ocean, nor the particles of water that spray about, though they appear separate, they remain one with the ocean.

According to a Jain maxim, *"He who conquers the sin of separateness conquers all other sins."*

1.4 QUANTUM GUILT: EXPLORING THREE TYPES OF GUILT

Guilt is rarely explored at the metaphysical level. For our purposes we will be looking at three types of guilt: Metaphysical, Existential and Psychological. Healing Quantum Guilt is based on guilt's origins as having been borne from the smallest possible beginning or singularity, which caused the perceived separation along with the concept of time and all of creation.

METAPHYSICAL GUILT (Unconscious)

Ontological guilt is the inherent price of the freedom of choice.
Kierkegaard

There's a deep unconscious feeling of guilt and wrongness in the mind that has not yet awakened and owes its existence to the belief that it is possible to separate from God. Because of that belief, sin and punishment naturally follow. There is a branch of Metaphysics called Ontology, that deals with the being itself at its core and the inherent cost of believing that we did indeed separate from Source. You might not know that you are affected by this "core" metaphysical guilt, but it is the motivating force behind your whole life. This core guilt makes you what you are and whatever is destined, at the time of the perceived separation, is carried with you. This core guilt shapes every aspect of our being, and we project it onto everything in our world, including our body. The ego is borne from this manifestation of our perceived separation from Source. All of our ills, relationship issues, conflicts and all modes of attack and cruelty arise out of the belief that we've separated from our Source, and so we must suffer. This is our core illusion and guilt is the glue that binds this world.

Metaphysical guilt is unconscious to us, so we don't feel it as guilt. For example, suppose you attend a powerful workshop, or have just spent some time with a great guru and you awaken to the truth of who you are – a complete and utter experience of your godliness. Then a few days later as you walk down the street, for no good reason, you feel like yelling at someone. You have no idea why you feel this way and you would never think of this feeling as guilt.

When we get close to the truth, we often feel the arising of this unconscious metaphysical guilt, as the ego doesn't like us to get close to freedom and truth because that would spell the end of its existence. The feelings that surface when we are close to the truth can be very uncomfortable and in blaming or attacking another, we in effect keep the guilt unconscious, and the ego gets to live another day. We immediately project these feelings outward onto everything and everyone making them the reason for our discomfort.

Metaphysical guilt arises from the deep belief that we have the power and the ability to split off from God or Source thus we believe that we have indeed split off. From this point on, we begin to experience great fear because we believe that we have done something horribly wrong for having left Source and we hate ourselves for it. Those who see God as punishing and vengeful will naturally feel afraid, fearful because they believe that God hates them for abandoning "Him". This perceived separation is carried in our psyche. The guilt that arises from the belief of separation is unconscious, and when it arises the first thing we want to do is to project it onto someone else so we can get rid of the awful feeling.

We believe we need to do this as quickly as possible before we are attacked by this punishing god that we've made up – it seems like we're all a little delusional. When an attacking feeling arises, instead of acting it out, you can say, "Hold on, something's coming up in me and I don't like how it feels." The fact that it is coming to your awareness is very good, because then the unconscious guilt can be seen and remedied before it attacks someone or something.

As long as we don't recognize this unconscious guilt, it will continue to unknowingly operate through us, as part of us thinks that if we project guilt outside of ourselves, guilt will be gone. But instead it will remain stuffed inside the unconscious mind, thereby allowing the belief in separation to be maintained.

The god that we are addressing isn't the real God but rather the ego camouflaging itself as the real God, but this ego only knows how to attack. It waits in hiding only to leap out at someone. We are always in conflict because the ego doesn't want us to recognize the unconscious guilt and wants to keep it hidden in our minds, and by not seeing it; we will continue to attack one another, thereby keeping the illusion of separation alive.

The only way that we can possibly release this ego game is to see that it runs us every moment of the day, even if we are spiritually advanced and as a result feel that we are more aware, we still have to go deeper. In spiritual groups, we project all of our love onto the teacher or the guru/master or God, which can be helpful because this projection gives us the opportunity to experience divine love. Placing all of our love onto one being doesn't always help us though, if we forget our oneness with each other, as it excludes all of the other beings that are a part of us.

The problem is that when the service, the satsang or the workshop is over, the love stops, as spiritual or religious groups don't necessarily stop our unconscious guilt; on the contrary, we innocently perpetuate this same pattern of attack by projecting the unconscious guilt onto fellow devotees, (other seekers), through our judgments and comparisons. And we feel justified in doing so because many of our teachers have not brought to our attention that all of our judgments, anger, fear and guilt are stemming from our belief in the core separation. And they may not have emphasized that everyone has to be seen as a divine being also. They do tell us that our reactions originate from our ego; however, we think that the ego belongs to us and that we are bad somehow. This only makes us feel worse because we appropriate it to ourselves. The problem is ego is a universal ego, not our personal individual flaw.

This thing called ego is only a symptom of our core separation, and is not who we truly are. If we are not aware of this, then we feel even more guilt, and we attack others and ourselves because we don't understand that we all are innocent and have never separated from Source in the first place, hence all are One. Thus, when we perform our many spiritual practices, such as chanting, meditation, study and seva, we must include all other beings (by seeing them as our own self), regardless of their attainments or levels. Otherwise our experiences won't lead us home. Instead we remain trapped inside a continuous spiral, cycling around and around all the while feeling bad about others and ourselves.

When we judge others we are in truth judging ourselves, which only prevents us from experiencing precisely what we want, perfect peace.

This is why we turn to masters such as Jesus, Buddha, Muhammad ... so we can realize that we've never left the oneness/Godhead – that we are still there, merged with the infinite. When we realize that we are all one, we see this unconscious guilt as an illusion brought about by a primal, metaphysical misunderstanding. The good news is that love is what is real and exists even deeper than the core of guilt and can dissolve all our illusions.

What is most tragically kept hidden ... is our unconscious guilt, which ... remains the stumbling block to our remembering our Creator and Source and the return home to His Love. (7)
Ken Wapnick

EXISTENTIAL GUILT

Metaphysical guilt is not felt as guilt because whenever we feel uncomfortable, we project it outward and while this might make our discomfort less, it only serves to keep the guilt hidden and unconscious. Whereas, Existential Guilt is felt as a deep suffering or longing. We often associate this existential guilt with neurosis or pathological guilt that is free-floating and attaches itself to many of our faults. When we correct one fault, the guilt simply jumps to another shortcoming, so we are never able to fully resolve the problem or fault.

Existential guilt does not respond to our attempts to change our behavior. No matter how good we become, we still feel guilty. Guilt works itself into our daily life and can arise at the slightest provocation. For instance, we can do a small and seemingly insignificant action that we might feel is improper, even after correcting it, this existential guilt can become overwhelming beyond belief.

Another element of this type of guilt is that it tends to follow us, and look for anything that it can find in order to make us feel guilty. It's like a sinking ship, as you try to patch one hole, two more appear. In addition, we may set very high standards for ourselves, which we will never be able to reach or maintain because we hope to find oneness and perfection in the world of form where only duality and separation seem to reign.

We all have Existential guilt lurking beneath the surface waiting to emerge. It takes over our whole being, when it finally does come out of the closet, it cannot be rectified with psychological techniques. This kind of guilt is the response to the unconscious guilt, as it knows that something is terribly wrong, yet it doesn't know what. And so this Existential guilt projects itself onto anything that it sees so it can feed the guilt and then punish itself thinking that guilt and punishment will appease the mind, but they never do.

Some feel that this Existential guilt is the core guilt, but in fact it is a symptom that has come into consciousness from the core guilt, (Metaphysical). We try to place our pain and guilt on the things in the outer, physical form, which is the very illusion itself. But this will not work as these feelings we project onto consciousness are themselves part of the illusion. Anything that appears in duality is illusory, including our separated consciousness, somewhat like dreaming.

All sorts of things take place in a dream that may be an expression of our pain and guilt, which we are trying to rid ourselves of. So we create numerous characters and situations to defend, fight, chase and so on – all of it seemingly very real and significant. But the problem is that we are the dream, the dreamer and the dreamed. However, there is an escape from our torment, we have to go beyond the dream to the core and see our separation from Source as the great illusion. Only then will we become free from Existential guilt or any other guilt for that matter.

PSYCHOLOGICAL GUILT

Psychological guilt is about our connection to the behaviors we judge, or that others judge, to be incorrect. Two statements that sum up psychological guilt are:

1/ "I did something that I shouldn't have."
2/ "I didn't do something that I should have."

The psychological model of guilt is sometimes entwined with our perception of love. We've grown up with family guilt, and guilt from those whom we look to for approval, as they've used guilt to manipulate us to behave and do the right thing. So guilt has become like an emotion that we've learned to live with, but it is not an emotion because emotions have positive and negative components to them. For instance, anger can be constructive in certain situations while guilt never really is. In fact it's been seen as the greatest obstacle to knowing who we are and keeps us from seeing others for who they truly are.

Guilt may be seen as a positive motivator, to do something you think is beneficial or to keep you from doing something that is not beneficial. But if action is motivated from guilt, the action won't be coming from your authentic self. If you are acting from guilt, you will feel resentment, because you don't really want to do the task, so you are not being true to yourself.

We generally withhold confessing to others, those things that we "think we should have done" or those things that we "think we shouldn't have done." But by expressing these withholds, to another trusted individual, we begin to loosen the tight grip – the habitual patterns that keep us in the guilt trap.

Everything that we try to do will only leave us with a temporary relief, because at the core, we still believe that we're separate from one another and ultimately from God. So no matter what we do in the form, to try to rid ourselves of the many feelings of guilt, nothing lasting will result because we are trying to change the reflection in the mirror when we should be taking our attention back to ourselves as this is where the reflection originates.

If there can be a positive aspect to guilt, it would be that it serves as a red flag, alerting us to the error of our perceptions. That's when life can become uncomplicated, as there would be only one choice to make; that being that we can choose to side with the ego, and believe the whole dream, (we call reality/world) to be real, or to choose to reunite with the truth of who we really are, this being that we are one with our Source, have never separated and are one with absolute love.

All forms of guilt are actually designed to keep us hurting and attacking, projecting our own inner conflict/war onto others or obsessing and hating ourselves, which often can make us ill. Sigmund Freud believed that there is an unconscious force, and unconscious sense of guilt within the individual that contributes to illness. He speaks of this unconscious sense of guilt as the most powerful of all obstacles to recovery.

So guilt has been working ceaselessly to keep us from remembering where our true home really is. Only when we stop running from the guilt and look at it clearly, do we have a chance of seeing through the illusion to the truth of who we truly are.

Most of your experiences are unconscious ...
Become aware of the unconscious ...
You cannot let go of something until you know what it is.
Nisargadatta Maharaj

1.5 WHAT IS GUILT?

If you did not feel guilty, you could not attack, for condemnation is the root of attack. It is the judgment of one mind by another as unworthy of love and deserving of punishment. (8)
A Course in Miracles

I have a client and friend whom I've worked with for many years. She is deeply spiritual and has a great desire to know her true nature. In our early work, she presented me with her feeling of being somehow "bad" or a "sinner." Over the years, we have explored her childhood, her father issues, etc. But as time passed, these feelings of "bad" and "guilty" persisted. They were like an invisible shroud over her whole life. To counter these feelings she tried to be more in control by obsessively busying herself with chores and activities. This was her attempt to deny the depth of pain that resulted from this deep sense of guilt. She eventually became discouraged. She felt stuck. She said, *"My wheels are spinning but I'm not getting anywhere."* She had stopped herself from feeling the one thing she wanted more than anything else – to experience her true, loving nature.

Then one day, as we were looking at this "bad" feeling and how it seeped into everything and every relationship in her life, I asked her, *"What is the real reason for this sense of sin?"* She thought for a while and then emphatically stated, *"I've done so many things in my life that I shouldn't have and have hurt so many people as a result because of my insensitivity. I find it extremely hard to live with myself. And by my having done these terrible things, I feel I have separated from God, and am not lovable. So I feel that I must be punished."*

In that moment, she recognized that this was the heavy shroud, which had permeated her whole life – a shroud of guilt. This was an important breakthrough because what followed was a very profound direct experience – that she was not a sinner at all, but pure love. This breakthrough occurred when she happened to glance at a memento, a glittering angel that one of her family members had lovingly given to her as a gift. This memento acted as a trigger that burst open the dam. She suddenly realized the truth, which had been hidden from her until that point. She saw how loved she really was by everyone in her life, which up until then she hadn't been able to feel let alone receive. But more importantly, she recognized her genuine goodness.

What followed was a vision of a stream of actions and inter-actions she had had with others that showed her just how much love and kindness was inherent despite her belief that she was bad and guilty. Then the perceived grievances, concerning friends and family, that she had held onto for many, many years, which only served to make her feel separate from and judgmental of everyone in her world, dissolved into love. Family and friends were no longer held in a negative light because she could now see their goodness and godliness and she had learned to recognize the goodness that also lay within her. After this realization, she wept with gratitude.

My friend saw in this experience that she is Love and that this is the only truth. All of the judgments and condemnations that she had about herself and others were illusory and simply false, having no basis in reality. After this, her relationships improved, and she saw that the life that she had been living was more like a bad dream that she had awakened from. She began to experience a new world based on love rather than guilt. Her sinful identity gradually changed and she became identified with the goodness and purity that we normally associate with God. She has been a great inspiration to me in writing this book.

What then, is this guilt/sin business? A Sikh saint says that it's about, *"Forgetting one's origin, (Godhead)."* The Buddhists refer to it as, *"Missing the mark."* A Persian mystic says that *guilt/sin or the world only comes into play when one forgets the Lord.* Kirpal Singh, a

Sant Mat master, says that, *"Sins, whether coarse or fine, are purely the invention of man under the sway of mind ... so long as a person acts as a self-willed creature; he subjects himself to all of the laws and their rigors."* A Course in Miracles says of sin/guilt, *" ... while you believe that your reality or your brother's is bounded by a body, you will believe in sin."*

A common theme is prevalent here. Guilt and Sin come into play when we forget who we really are; it is here an illusion is created, forming a reality that we believe to be true. We then believe we are a body that does all actions, and are thus subject to all of the laws of the world and their consequences.

In this state we separate ourselves from our true source by perceiving a reality, based on the duality of "self" and "other." We see only a body that commits bad actions and therefore deserves to be punished in some way, because we think that we are just a body that is subject to all of the laws of the world and its rigors, i.e. Karma, (cause and effect). Then this split or belief in being a body, hence the doer of actions, is like the kingpin from which springs all of the so-called seven deadly sins: greed, lust, pride, wrath, envy, sloth and gluttony. I would add an eighth as well, blame. So in essence, this world we call "reality" emanates from the one perceived major, so-called sin, that being the belief in separation from Source, and this goes hand-in-hand with guilt.

Guilt constantly haunts us because deep down inside we believe that we are separate from our source, from others and our self because we see ourselves as merely these physical bodies rather than divine beings that emanate the light that is our true nature.

This is the real reason we feel guilt so deeply, we feel that we have somehow offended or hurt God, so we project our guilt onto "Him" by turning "Him" into a punishing god. So much so that we hide away in our darkness, away from the light, just so we can suffer from our self-imposed punishment thereby saving "Him" the trouble of punishing us.

It is guilt and separation that makes a person judge or harm another. Big or small sins are really the same in that they all originate from the same source – illusion – that stems from the belief that we are separate from Source and therefore we are bad and expect to be punished. When we look out from our physical eyes, all we see are our projections of our own guilt – this original belief in separation, which permeates everything. At this stage we have not yet learned, or rather, remembered that we are one with everything and that all we see are our projections. We see projections of guilt, and shortcomings in others, we then judge them, or in some cases harm them, physically, mentally or emotionally, that is, when we're not preoccupied with doing that to ourselves.

When we miss the mark or break the law, we make the error of believing in the wrong reality. When we believe in this wrong reality, which is the result of separation from Divine source, we experience many debilitating feelings such as unworthiness, doubt, guilt, pride, and anger, to name only a few. We then project these often-unconscious feelings onto others; moreover, we may even blame them for our mess. Wars are waged because we truly believe there is another person, group, or even an entire country of threatening people to fight against. We may see these groups as "sinners" and believe that once we win the war, we'll be at peace again, having regained our land or oil or whatever the issue. All crimes originate from this sense of separation, which in our world ultimately leads to punishment. But if we were able to catch ourselves when we begin to see ourselves in the light of guilt, then by remembering our godliness/goodness, we could return to our true source where nothing exists but love. Once we remember who we really are, which is one with the divine, we could not commit a sinful act or crime, because we would be seeing everyone in the light of purity, oneness and innocence and that any harm that we inflict against another is really only an act of harm against our own selves. Remember the old adage, "Peace begins with me."

I recall hearing about a tribe in Africa, whose members would deal with punishment in a completely different and unique way. They would gather together and form a circle, with the so called "sinner" sitting in the middle and then every person in the circle would in turn say something positive or good about this guilty person. This would continue until everyone in the circle was able to express a positive and uplifting aspect of this person with the end result being that the "sinner" would realize his inherent goodness and would reform himself much more quickly than if he were punished and made to feel guilty.

This approach could also be applied to the children in our schools. If we could strive to inculcate in them a sense of self-love and respect rather than guilt, sin, jealousy and so on, they would learn at an early age that if they were to hurt another that they were also harming themselves and conversely, when they empower another they are also empowering themselves. In this way, we could make a fundamental change in future generations, eliminating violence and war by stopping self-hatred within the individual first.

When the Buddhists find the chosen child who is believed to be the incarnation of a previous great being, they begin to treat him like a god and train him to be a noble, just and compassionate leader of their people. This child is taught to identify himself as a divine being who is ultimately one with all others. However, I firmly believe that if we all could treat our children as a god, with respect and honor and teach them to be compassionate, loving and just, then our children could be just as noble as the "chosen one" for they too would see their oneness with all of life and all people.

It is important to remember that as long as we think there is "another," out there somewhere, there will always be war and conflict. We are all just one being in many forms, and any attempt at killing another ends with us killing that part of ourselves, ensuring that no peace can ever exist. It's not unlike looking into a mirror and hating what you see or feel or think, and then smashing the mirror hoping that the pain goes away. But there will always be another mirror to reflect our wrong under-standings, which in essence is just another opportunity to make the necessary correction in our perspective/outlook and to see with the right vision.

He that is conscious of guilt cannot bear the innocence of others: So they will try to reduce all others to their own level.
Charles James Fox

1.6 UPSET FOR THE WRONG REASON

Recently, I found myself grieving for my ex-husband whom I was married to over three decades ago. I came to completion with him many, many years ago and both of us have moved on. In fact I feel like I've lived ten lifetimes since the marriage. But one day, his image showed up in my mind and I was propelled into my past. There I was, suddenly longing to return to my old life with him, and I found myself sobbing with guilt for having left him.

Days went by and this grief and pain for my ex-husband became unbearable, and I felt I would die. So I sat down and asked myself questions such as, *"Would I really go back?" "No"* was my answer. And as I kept questioning myself about him, I slowly realized that this longing wasn't about him at all. It was about the pain that I've carried inside. Ever since I was a baby, I remember standing up in a crib, howling at the darkness with the same pain as I was now feeling and projecting onto my ex-husband. So I dissolved his image and just let myself feel the pain. I began to pray – "Please help me feel the love that I really am, instead of this painful separation."

The answer to my prayer revealed that the heartbreak and suffering in my lifetime had nothing to do with 'others' or 'situations,' because the same pain was underlying all my interactions. My broken heart originated inside of me. I stayed with this feeling of grief for what I thought was for my ex-husband, and after a while, like a soft breeze, I began to feel the love that I am, and always have been. I recognized that the grief we feel is never for the person or the situation, but is for the deep feeling of separation from our true Source, which results in the feeling of a profound lack of love. When we split with a loved one, we go right back to the terrible suffering of the unconscious guilt. All of our suffering can be traced back to the belief that we separated from our source. However, in truth we have always been with our Divine Self in all situations whether we believed it or not. This is why understanding of the core guilt can return us to the place where we are already and have always been one with our Creator. Love is what we are and no form of separation can remove love from us.

We can come to recognize that all suffering, all loss and every sort of abandonment, immediately propels us back to the belief of the original separation from our Source. Many teachers, gurus and scriptures tell us that we are, *"Living in a dream world"* and we need to *"Wake up!"* In other words, this world that we take to be true and real is itself a dream and any and all pain and suffering we may experience is part of the dream. But whether we are awake or asleep, we are loved eternally. We are with the Absolute's love always, a love that has never left us. It is only when we believe ourselves to be only this body that we seem to inhabit, therefore real and separate beings, and this world to be real and true, that we will feel the fear of having no love. Life is infinitely simpler, when you no longer need to analyze yourself or try to figure out your feelings, your childhood, your fears and especially your guilt and align with who you truly are.

All we need to know is there is only ever one thing happening – eternal love – and anytime we find ourselves suffering over anything at all, it is always our unconscious guilt and the pain of our belief of our separation from Source. We can use the soul's longing as a beacon to find our way back "home" where we are one with Love. By saying, *"I'm sorry, I forgot that I am already one with you Spirit,"* then we can drop out of our involvement with conflict and doership and return back to our true self and rest in the lap of the Divine.

Your prayer to God is only God praying to Himself.
Wayne Liquorman

1.7 THE LAST ILLUSION

While watching a video of the well-known Indian epic, *The Mahabharata*, which is essentially about the conflict or Great War between two families, the Pandavas, who lived a life of Dharma (righteousness or forces of good), and their cousins the Kauravas, who were seen to represent Adharma (unrighteousness or forces of evil); I was struck by the last segment, which made reference to the final illusion. The ending was unexpected, and at the time, this twist was a hard one for me to wrap my mind around.

The story is narrated by Veda Vyasa, who is the Divine Guru in the story. In the last segment, "The Final Illusion," the eldest Pandava brother, Yudishthira (also seen as the incarnation of Dharma – the good guy), took the 'Great Journey' north with his family to the polar mountain, which led to the heavenly world, believing it was time for them to depart from this realm. One by one they all died along the way, as was the intention. Yudishthira reaches the gates of heaven, together with a dog that he befriends on the journey. At this juncture, in order to gain permission to enter Heaven, he is asked to leave the dog behind, but he would not abandon his new companion. He turns away from Heaven, and as he begins to leave, Vyasa tells him the dog was but another form of Dharma and calls him back.

Arriving in heaven, Yudishthira is simply aghast when he finds his mortal enemy Duryodhana, along with all of his family residing in heaven seemingly joyous and carefree. At this point, Vyasa instructs Yudishthira to embrace Duryodhana, saying, *"Here is where all hate vanishes. Kiss him."* But Yudishthira can't reconcile this and wants to see his own family, who are not there. *"What is paradise if I'm separated from my family?"* He then asks Vyasa, *"Where is my family?"* Vyasa tells him that they are someplace else and escorts him into hell.

As he descends into the horror of hell, he hears his family

calling to him. *"You're here?"* he calls back. *"Tortured, in this rotten smell of corpses? Who decided this? Am I awake? What act have you, my good family, committed to be thrown down into hell?"* Yudishthira makes a decision. *"I condemn the gods; I condemn Dharma! I'll stay here in hell forever, to be with my family."* Then there was a great emptiness. Finally, the "keeper" of this last dwelling place spoke to Yudishthira and said, *"You've known neither paradise nor hell. Here,* (in this place of non-duality) *there is no happiness, no punishment, no family, and no enemies. Rise in tranquility. Here words end in the thought with which they began. All actions, good or bad disappear. This is your final illusion."*

To most, this story would not make logical sense. Are we not taught that if our actions are noble and good, we'll go to heaven, and if our actions are bad we'll get a one-way ticket to hell? But in this epic story, which is one of the most significant Indian teachings, we are shown that Heaven and Hell are illusions and that we must rise in tranquility beyond the confines of these dualistic worlds to the realm where opposites – happy/sad, good/bad, paradise/hell, friend/enemy – do not exist, and where no words or thoughts exist either.

Yudishthira was the epitome of Dharma. The Mahabharata, the "great war," was essentially about the battle between good and evil. But all of this is acknowledging the belief in duality, that there actually is a friend or a foe, and that in vanquishing "evil," victory, peace, and even salvation can be attained. Yet here, at the end of the saga, they introduce the idea that *all* forms of opposites – good/bad, righteous/unrighteous, Heaven/Hell – are themselves not real, but merely illusions.

We could compare this state to a dream where the events and characters seem real enough as long as the dreamer is asleep and involved in the drama, but after they awaken they are able to recognize that it was all only a dream. Many saints and mystics often tell their students, *"Wake up! This world is not real … it is but a dream!"* Thus, one interpretation of what Vyasa is saying is that once we "wake up" from believing this world / reality to be real, we too will see that we were simply asleep and this dream that we call reality, never happened. We can then join the place of union with the divine beyond the limitations of thoughts, concepts, and dualities.

In this place, nothing of this illusion has been born and nothing has separated, so we have not sinned. Guilt is the father of illusion, and the body/mind and all of its actions, good or bad, arise only in this "so called" reality/dream and are punished and praised here also. But when we rise beyond this dream, we have pulled the cord on "guilt – our last illusion" and we are left innocent and free.

"There is no world," therefore "forsake all Dharmas."
The Diamond Sutra

PART II

HOW GUILT TRAPS US

2.1 THE INVISIBLE SHROUD

Some would argue that guilt does not affect them and is only for the religiously minded. Many would insist they are their own person guided by their own morality and ethics, and besides, they'd point out and question, *"What about the real sinners – murderers, rapists, and pedophiles?"*

These sorts of questions and attitudes arise from the belief that we are unconnected from one another. This common perspective owes its existence to the ego's denials of unity and oneness. This denial is what forms an invisible shroud over our eyes, hearts and soul, which only serves to keep us blinded to the truth while believing the lies of the world. At the absolute level of reality, which is where we really live (our true home), and of which we are mostly not conscious, the only thing that exists is love and it is here that we are sinless. At the relative level, our everyday world (the world that we think we see and believe to be real) is only a dream based on the belief that we have separated from our true home. Here, we experience the nightmare of guilt. We dream we have separated from our source and are therefore sinners. The truth is that we have never left our source, and we are innocent and pure.

In effect, this view is completely opposite to what we've been conditioned to believe – what we consider "real" is in fact, a dream. The purpose of this book is not to make excuses for criminals or to absolve them of their crimes, because in this physical realm, sin and punishment do exist and harming another can never be justified. Ultimately, in order to stop abuses and other atrocities we have to stop our own many little "murders" – of others and ourselves – in our everyday lives. Everything originates from us, and therefore becomes our world and affects our world. If destructive people are in our world, it is only because they are a part of us – a part in need of forgiveness.

Perhaps this view sounds extreme, but if we would take just a few moments to watch how we commit these many little murders by seeing how much we judge others and ourselves in numerous small ways, be it directly or just in our minds, we would likely be very surprised.

Also, we might notice an underlying sense of guilt when thinking, *"I've done something I shouldn't have,"* or *"I haven't done something that I should have."* We berate ourselves incessantly, often unconsciously, with this sort of thinking. When we've exhausted the self-flagellation, we take that fatal next step and project our low-grade judgment and guilt onto some unsuspecting person, such as a cab driver, cashier, receptionist, waiter, our spouse, our children, the government and even another race, minority or country. Anything is fair game for release. We may feel relieved for a moment when we blame others because we seem free from our sense of sin and torment for a short while, but then someone says something to trigger us and before long, this low-grade, unconscious self-doubt and guilt begins to stir within us again.

We get angry, we might have a drink to numb ourselves or to give us courage, we might curse our lot in life, or we might simply deny that anything is happening at all. These "solutions" will only lead to obsessive thoughts bubbling up inside, such as wondering what we're going to eat next, who we're going to sleep with, who we hate and would like to blame our troubles on or maybe even get rid of if we could. We might head to the medicine cabinet to pop a pill in order to temporarily relieve the emptiness and depression that we've been subject to for so long.

These behaviors are common in today's world. Yet we are surprised when someone we know has a slip – they can no longer keep up their façade of *"everything is fine!" "What went wrong?"* we ask, but we don't have to look very far for the answer. We only need look more deeply within ourselves, where we will see the pain that we humans bear in our deepest, darkest moments, pain that cries out, *"I'm not enough, I'm not worthy, I feel this endless, empty hole, and I'll never be good enough to crawl out. I've sinned somehow, God must hate me, this is why I must suffer, and I can't tell anyone, because they won't understand ..."*

We feel we can't reveal our malaise to anyone, because we believe they will simply deny it and tell us to think positively, and then they'll smile to hide the shameful sin that we all carry. We prefer to live in denial of the amount of guilt and fear that exists within us rather than live in our hearts, where we are held in forgiveness and love. But of course, living in our hearts is much harder to do, because we would need to see guilt for what it is – the biggest lie of all, an invisible shroud casting despair on our lives. For example, we all know some people who flippantly use phrases like, *"It's all good,"* or *"This too shall pass,"* or some other phrase that is unconnected to what they are feeling. These phrases minimize the intensity of the pain, partly because they know that others may not be interested in hearing their problems and partly because they feel ashamed at even having feelings of pain or angst in the first place.

And we may notice that as a result of denying feelings, we feel that the human/heart connection is severed, and then we feel excluded or separate from others even more. When we cut ourselves off from our true feelings, we are in turn cutting others off from connecting with us. We're left feeling more alone and despondent. This is what the ego wants us to feel so as not to break free of the invisible shroud of guilt.

All our suffering arises from our belief that we are just this body-mind that is the doer. And we believe that our actions lead to guilt, but on the contrary, guilt is an extremely deep program in our unconscious that is reinforced from our birth and pervades our entire life. Guilt will control us until we discover its origin.

Our actions have nothing to do with causing guilt since guilt is already deeply embedded within us. Actions can be changed and yet we may notice that guilt just keeps on going, despite the changes that we've instituted. This is because there is something else that we feel guilty about all of the time that has nothing to do with our actions. All guilts are actually symptoms of the deep metaphysical guilt, which is the belief that we've separated from Source.

Somewhere deep inside ourselves, we know where we truly live, and more importantly who we are, and we will never be at peace until we can settle into our true home, where guilt, blame or projection of any kind does not exist. There is a story of a lion cub that strayed from its den and took up with a herd of sheep. The herd accepted the cub as one of their own and over time the cub matured and thrived. However, it thought it was also a sheep. Then, one day, an adult lion was surveying the land from a hilltop and was curious as to why this young lion was playing with the sheep rather than eating them. He approached it and asked why. The young lion said that he too was a sheep. Then the older lion took him to a pond and made him look at his reflection, so that he would see that he was in fact, a lion, a king. We too must see who we truly are. When we identify ourselves as just a body/personality, we have limited our greatness that extends far beyond anything we can see with our physical eyes.

2.2 THE "SHOULD HAVES" THAT MURDER

We are our own greatest judge and jury. We live in a sea of "should haves" and "shouldn't haves." In fact, these "shoulds," in their various forms, direct our lives. It's somewhat like having a nagging spouse on our case 24/7, harping at us with, *"You shouldn't have done that!"* or *"You really should do this."* But this scenario is not restricted to spouses. Anyone can play this role for us – friend, parent, co-worker, or colleague – and it is no surprise that we attract such negative people into our lives because they are simply mirroring the fact that we are also constantly nagging at ourselves.

We may feel at times as though we've been implanted with a self-torture mechanism based on guilt, and presented with so many concerns and ideals about how we should live. These implants dictate how we should act, how we should look, how much money we should make, how many kids we should have, how often we should have sex, what we should eat – the list is endless. Our family is the first, but by no means the last group to implant us with their ideas or beliefs about what and whom we should value, and what and whom we should judge and hate. These applied beliefs are not just toward the world in general, but more damagingly, to our self-esteem, our core values, which leads to the disempowerment of our soul.

Added to that dangerous mix of "shoulds" are the various forms of media that influence us constantly, from a very young age and throughout our lives. Television, movies, magazines, and of course the Internet are all conspiring to indoctrinate us by affirming what we should look like, feel like, and what we should be doing in order to live happily – not to mention what we should buy in order to achieve that. Our governments continually try to sway us into following their party lines to have us see their version of the "right direction." Friends and partners always seem to know the "right thing" for us, even though it seems they rarely truly listen to us. Religious groups and organizations act as though they have an inside connection with God and they instruct us about "Him" and what we "should" do to appease "Him" or get into "His" good books, but this is only their opinion, their projection.

Is it any wonder that we spend so much time wondering what we should or should not do? These "shoulds" stem from all those past indoctrinations, acting as justifications for making many wrong decisions in our life, such as *"I should have married someone else"* or *"I should have done a business degree instead of psychology"* or *"I should have been there when my father died."* Shoulds also greatly influence our current decisions for our future.

Our regrets are the "should haves" of our past. These "should haves" then reach into the future and plan a course for us, and if we don't follow it, we feel bad, guilty, or like a failure. What's most difficult for us to see is that the ego is conspiring against and enshrouding the truth with this should/guilt/Sin business. The ego is in denial of our inner turmoil. This denial is one of should/sin/Guilt's most treasured soldiers because it keeps the war going within us, hence in our world. If we were to look at the inner war that is constantly waging, we might begin to question it: *"Hey, what kind of game are we playing here?"* We might even decide to delete those old programs of belief in guilt, sin and separation – that the ego has used to murder our true selves – thereby releasing the guilt that we've carried all our lives and reclaiming our souls. Only then can we birth ourselves into the love and innocence that is our birthright. Deciding to delete those old programs might seem like a daunting task, and it is.

But by forgiving these old programs, we are able to release them and replace them with a correct vision, that of our oneness with the Divine.

Love of the Self eliminates concern with anything else; it is without attachment. You are that love that is formless, nameless and indestructible.

Nisargadatta Maharaj

2.3 LOVE GONE WRONG

It's no accident that three-fourths of our TV shows feature characters in crisis looking for contentment, love, and resolution. We are those TV characters, we know when we're trapped, and we know we've got to escape from this melodrama we're starring in and return to peace and love. However, everyday life doesn't always work that smoothly as it does in a one-hour TV program.

One reason for this constant drama and entrapment is that we're seeking love in the wrong places; I call this "love gone wrong." This drama prevents us from finding the love we seek, which is why we continue to chase our proverbial tails in this incessant search. We chase wealth, sex, power, beauty, security, fame, recognition, and so on. However, we unconsciously chase all these elusive material objects and desires that only lead us to an ego-based love. What we seek is real love, (love of our true self), this love can never be tarnished or taken from us, nor can it be bought, sought or manifested as it's already within us, it's already ours!

This chasing cycle continues because we need to feel love at any cost; we are caught in it and controlled – prisoners of ourselves – our collective addiction. Addictions originate from the idea of sin because they produce guilt. Somewhere deep in our unconscious we believe that we have separated from our true source and hence are separate from one another. This is what we've been conditioned to believe from a very early age, to see the differences rather than the similarities however, very few of us have ever questioned whether this was indeed a valid perspective.

Only the enlightened ones have had the courage to step forth and offer us the alternative to this lie of separation. We never question the lie; so we live the lie and obsess about our sins, thereby replacing God and love with sin and guilt. Truth is always extremely simple. Where we place our attention, is what we become. If you put your focus on sin, you become a sinner and your world reflects that. By placing your focus on God, you become divine, and you see the world from a divine perspective.

Focusing on our sense of separation or sinfulness makes us look to the material aspects of the world for love because we've given our greatest gift away: our true power, our oneness with the eternal. We trade in diamonds for rhinestones. But thankfully we know, deep in our hearts that we've never separated from our true self but in believing that we had, we have replaced real love with ego love. The problem is that ego love is temporal and therefore, impermanent, whereas true love is eternal and never changes.

All addiction is the ego's attempt to replace God with itself – "love gone wrong". Real love would have us see and be the truth. Ego love is not love at all, because it only leads to chaos and frustration and certainly doesn't allow for us to experience peace or reveal our best selves. In fact, what is referred to, as ego love, is only another addiction, where we project the divine qualities of real love onto the impermanent things of the world. Imagine being desperately thirsty, and someone gives you a photograph of a glass of water instead of the real thing, a poor replacement indeed.

Addictions and concepts perpetuate the endless cycle of illusion. If we were to return to our true nature, there would be no need for this game. Fortunately, there is a way out, by seeing that everything is love, in either a contracted or expanded form. Where we go wrong, is when we choose to believe that the impermanent world is real – a world that not only gives us nothing of lasting value, but also is finite. This is the contracted form of love. But in the expanded form, love can raise us up above the trivialities of our current existence and bring us to an awareness of perfection, peace, and oneness with the divine.

In the expanded state, we are able to embrace the truth – that we are one with all that is/Divine Source, and have never separated. Instead we are living in a dream from which we need only to "awaken" in order to reclaim our birthright. When we see everything as love, we take a step outside of the illusion and see illusion for the game that it is. For instance, rather than looking upon an action as being either bad or sinful, it can be seen as the soul's cry for help and love.

We look for love or joy or even God on the outside, not unlike the musk deer that lives in the Himalayan Mountains. As the deer matures into adulthood, a gland in its naval begins to emit the smell of musk. The deer then becomes obsessed with this sweet smell of musk and begins to seek its source everywhere, outside of its own self, completely unaware that its source is from its own naval. So too, we are completely unaware that the source of love or joy and Divinity is already within us.

Sri Ramakrishna, a famous mystic of 19th-century India, had often been quoted as saying, *"The more you focus on sin, the more you become a sinner. The more you focus on God, then you become one with That."*

When we focus on the dream of sin and guilt, we can never do anything right. You win, and then lose; we achieve something only to lose it; we struggle helplessly against oppressors. We just can't come out victorious. People at their death who are still attached to the world of limitations and illusion feel tremendous guilt for not completing something or still desire to do more, or they regret having done it all wrong.

I have a wonderful friend, one of the most talented people I know and probably one of the most selfless. She creates brilliant works of art and uses her talents to serve others limitlessly. One day, I was acknowledging her for her gifts, and she confided in me. She felt that not only was she not good enough, but she also somehow wasn't doing enough, that she needed to do more. In that moment I saw the destructive pattern that she was caught in. Her unconscious mind was repeating the self-defeating mantra,

"If I really try hard, perhaps I can be free of my daily torment, and perhaps God will love me then." We then work harder but feel as though we're not doing enough, not being a good enough parent, or a good enough student, or spouse, or provider, or devotee of our spiritual teacher, and so on. We feel inherently bad in some way.

Because we feel bad, we want others to feel bad as well, and we end up holding others in a place of darkness with condemnation and self-righteousness. This punishment that we constantly seek for others and ourselves keeps sin alive. We treat self-flagellation, or false humility, with misplaced respect, and we honor its power. In fact, we worship this judgment and see it as true and real, and because we think that it is real, we can't release it and end up, self-righteously, projecting this judgment onto others, making them feel bad.

Matthew Fox, a great scholar and priest, wrote a profoundly moving book entitled *Original Blessing* that spoke about the divinity and joy of our birth rather than the original sin of our birth. I heard he was excommunicated shortly thereafter, a perfect example of love gone wrong. I also heard that he refused to acknowledge this, by saying, *"I belong to no one but God, so I cannot be excommunicated."*

Most of us would travel to the ends of the earth to be acknowledged in some way, but what we're asking for is to be seen for the part of us that is love and innocence rather than as damaged, guilty or not good enough. Because we are generally never seen in the highest light, we feel badly about ourselves. We unconsciously believe that we've done something wrong so we try harder to be good, but guilt attracts us to the kingpin that everything twirls on – Sin, because guilt has an obsessive quality, which focuses tirelessly on our faults and that causes us to believe that we've sinned or erred in some way. This idea of sin seems more real to us than our purity and our innocence. We are controlled by sin and therefore unable to experience our true nature, (love), which is why guilt is sin's right-hand man, as guilt keeps us constantly attracted to sin and not the other way around. For sin to continue to exist and thereby keep this dream world/illusion alive, it needs guilt. So our guilt is constantly thinking about the wrong actions that we've committed, whether we are conscious of these actions or not, and we keep monitoring ourselves as to whether we are performing good or bad actions rather than thinking about or identifying with our innocence, purity and oneness with our Divine Self.

Understanding the difference between focusing only on our bad actions versus placing our attention on ourselves as a pure part of God is the key that can set us free. For example, we're directed by our religious and spiritual paths to perform good actions, to eat in certain ways and purify our ego. Some of us are given spiritual names like, "Ram" or "Bhakti," which represent aspects of the divine/God so that we can reinforce our connection with our higher self. We are suffused with countless rituals and rites to help us avoid bad actions thereby avoiding bad karma. The problem is that we'll never purify the ego because it comes from the hidden illusion of sin/separation in the first place and from this illusion comes all of the seven deadly sins; pride, envy, lust, greed, anger, gluttony and sloth and their many variations. All of this cleansing and purification is good up to a point; however, cleansing simply serves to perpetuate this belief in the dream of sin. If we didn't feel that we were so impure in the first place, we wouldn't have to work so hard to clean ourselves up. Our belief in sin traps us in an endless cycle while never setting us free. This is how religious organizations and governments control us. But nothing can control us when we live in our pure egoless self.

I remember listening to a talk by Maharaj Ji, a modern day "saint" who said something very profound about this very issue, it never left me. He asked, *Why do we keep trying to clean up the slums, why not just move to the castle?* A simple shift in perception in which we begin to identify ourselves as already pure rather than sinful, unforgivable and needing to constantly purge ourselves of impurities, can have us living in the castle.

I have a friend who gets very upset when I speak like this. She insists that if we don't keep focused on our bad behaviors and try to keep them in check, then everyone would be unkind or harmful to others. My response to her is quite the contrary. If we identify with our innocence, purity and inherent goodness, then we are seeing through the eyes of love and therefore, we see the very best in others since we are recognizing that in ourselves first. Unfortunately, we see ourselves as wretched beings that need to be punished or on the contrary, we see ourselves as better than others. So by seeing through the eyes of judgment and ego, we see the worst in others because we see that in ourselves as well.

What makes sin and guilt so attractive is that it is something that we carry deep in our unconscious mind and sin's right-hand man – guilt – keeps us addicted to sin. As long as we feel like a sinner, we need to purify this wrong belief through various practices until we can become aware of the magnificent love we already are.

We'll never be at peace as long as we're seeking love, from the wrong sources. The Buddhists refer to the placing of one's attention on the world (love gone wrong) rather than on source as, "missing the mark." So to "hit the mark" would require us to turn our attention back to source, thereby making love go right.

2.4 WHY GUILT TRAPS US

I recall sharing a room with a beautiful young woman who had great devotion to God in her heart. We were in a spiritual ashram /monastery doing Seva (selfless service), contemplation, yoga, and meditation. People came from all over the world to see the spiritual master/guru with the hopes of furthering their evolvement. I knew that this young woman was a stripper in her life outside the ashram, but I thought nothing of it until one day I walked into our room and found her sobbing. I asked her what was wrong. She revealed that she wanted to be close to the master but some of the others ostracized, judged, and discouraged her from seeking out the master because in their eyes she was impure. She went on to say that she was not accepted in the ashram and that God must really hate her.

I could see how absurd her thinking was, so I embraced her and told her in a very strong voice, "God doesn't care if you strip. "He" doesn't even see your perceived sins. All "He" sees is the oneness of your spirit with "His", your perfection, and your love. You are love – please don't forget that! You are not your physical body or your personality." Some part of her heard me very deeply. I'll never forget the joy and gratitude she expressed to me for our moment, and her return to her real self – glowing with the conviction of truth in her heart.

> Every Saint has a past, every sinner a future.
> Kirpal Singh

Sin is a remarkably effective mechanism to control us and can do so only because we forget that we *are* inherently good, just as we *are* already with God, whether we can feel it or not. So if we do something inappropriate to others or to ourselves, we will punish others or ourselves so we both suffer, all in the name of sin and guilt, and yet all the while thinking that what we are doing is right. This is a self-imposed system and not forced upon us by God. Why this system works so well is because we are love in our essence, we feel guilty when we do an action, which we consider to be sinful, so we punish ourselves. The ensuing guilt keeps us continually repeating the same cycles of sin and punishment, which become an addictive behavior. Sin needs guilt or it will dissolve. Instead of seeing our actions as sinful and being guilty, if we could correct at the root, our wrong action, and to see it as needing to be corrected rather than something to feel guilt about, (which would inevitably lead to some form of punishment), then we could begin to be free of this addiction.

We think that God is somewhere far away and has nothing better to do but to sit in judgment of our sins. We fail to under-stand that harsh treatment toward others and ourselves is exactly what distances us from our true self and God.

We are conditioned to believe that God will love us if we are good, and judge us if we are bad, but how can a perfect God treat us in such a conditional way? Is this not the behavior of a tyrant? The god of this world has us in his snare as long as we believe that we are sinners. We can be freed from his reign of tyranny when we wake up to our absolute innocence and purity. This is why great beings bring this wisdom to us, by teaching us that our true nature, is already one with the true God. The true God does not see sin nor require punishment. However, the god of this made up world uses sin and punishment to keep us bound by having us believe that we are just a body and the doer of all actions. This then leads to the erroneous belief that we must suffer and therefore be punished. As long as we think and act from our ego, which is synonymous with doership, (the belief that we alone do everything without our divine self), we will feel bad and guilty. This only serves to keep us feeling small and separate from God and each other. But we need to learn that we are really beings of light who want to love one another. As long as we think this illusion is real, and as long as we feel that we have done something that does not fit our standards of goodness, we will hold back and not allow ourselves to experience our true nature.

Experiencing our true nature can happen in an instant. Typically, we start off believing that we are "bad" or impure then over time, we realize we do have some redeeming qualities – so we're not, "all that bad." Then we might have an "Aha" moment when we see past the veil of illusion to our truth. This "Awakening" opens up our awareness so that we can see the world for what it is, an illusion. Then we begin to deepen or strengthen our knowing, our conviction of whom we truly are, thus loosening the binds that have enslaved us to the lies of the world.

Here we are more readily able to catch ourselves when we slip and get caught in the outer world of illusions and lies by remembering who we truly are, thereby returning to the peace, love and safety of our God-Self ... where there is no "Other," no "Victim," and ultimately no "Me." A Buddhist meditation master, Chogyam Trungpa Rinpoche had said, *"Enlightenment is the ego's ultimate disappointment."*

In order to facilitate the journey of self-discovery, spiritual teachers have us perform actions and practices that help us feel good about ourselves and consequently allow us to experience our real selves. The great beings teach us to live by the rules – but to stay focused only on God – in order to become free.

However, great beings know they are beyond karma. Karma was established as the law of the physical realm to mete out the appropriate reaction to our actions. Lord Krishna, in the Bhagavad Gita describes this concept in the following way. When we do good actions, we create good karma, these are seen as golden chains and when we do bad actions, we create bad karma and these in turn are seen as iron chains.

The problem is that they are both chains that bind us to where we must experience the fruits of our actions – both good and bad. Ideally, if we can go beyond the duality of sin we can live in a state free of karma, at one with our true God-self. I recall hearing Irina Tweedie, the author of *Chasm of Fire*; say that her master had told her, "*For you there is karma, but not for me.*" He knew that he was one with love/God and that she was still identified as the "doer," (the "I" that thinks it makes it all happen). Therefore, as long as she believed that she was separate from God and subject to the laws of karma, she would feel eternally guilty. If there were one kingpin to rend the illusion of separation, it would be non-doership.

Most of us are trapped by this addiction to sin and guilt because we deeply believe we are a body and personality that is doing some action – good or bad. As Kirpal Singh says in his book, *The Wheel of Life*, "*As long as one acts as a self-willed creature, he subjects himself to all the laws and their rigors.*" (9) However, the corollary to this is that when one surrenders himself completely to God, he naturally becomes free of the disease of sin and the karma because he is no longer living in the world of the ego but rather in God's world.

It is time for us to question this deep, unconscious belief that we are inherently bad, to see if it is really true. Then when we finally discover that the belief is empty, we can begin to put our focus on our Godliness rather than on our sinfulness.

Unlike the true God, the god of this world gives us laws so thorough and intricate that no one can escape from them on their own. These laws lack compassion, using everything possible to keep us cycling back to the illusion/dream of separation and the burden of repetitive existence. Our sin and virtue cannot be questioned or balanced in a loving way, because karma is based on fear. Imagine a terrifying parent keeping you locked in a basement, creating rules that are like walking in a minefield – you just tiptoe along, hoping the explosive is not under your next step. Your parent tells you that if you take one wrong step, you will be punished, and from then on you will never be free to repeat the experience in a positive way. Or, if you do act properly, you will still never be allowed out of the basement. Your parent also binds you in another way because you must return to his domain to reap any rewards. All the rules are his; so long as we believe in "good" or "bad", "right" or "wrong", no thought is given to your soul's desire to return to its true home with God and love.

2.5 HOW WE USE GUILT TO TRAP ONE ANOTHER

The Negro needs the white man to free him from his fear.
The White man needs the Negro to free him from his guilt.
Martin Luther King Jr.

My mother was raised in a rural environment and attended a Catholic school. On a regular basis, and for no good reason, my mother was beaten by nuns. The teachings of guilt and sin were used to keep the children in line. At the tender age of twelve, her parents also put her to work, as both of her younger brothers had recently died from cancer and the family needed income. My mother suffered from lifelong unworthiness and guilt for having been the sole healthy survivor in the family.

Predictably, as her first child, I was the recipient of her pain. Every day I would tiptoe down the stairs, terrified, and pray that Mom was still in bed. If she wasn't in bed, she'd be waiting at the kitchen table for me so she could project her unconscious guilt and unworthiness onto me, which made her feel better about herself. *"You disgust me,"* was her morning greeting. This kind of behavior intensified as I was approaching age twelve and becoming a young woman. I was made to feel great shame and guilt, simply for being alive, just as she had felt.

Eventually, I lost all confidence and became very shy; I was afraid that all of my actions were somehow sinful and unacceptable. I lost faith in myself. I recall looking at a photo album at that time and seeing pictures of myself at the age of four, noticing how vibrant and alive I was. But by the time I was twelve, my young eyes were dull with confusion, sadness, and guilt.

As the years progressed, I stumbled through life, studying psychology and dance, taking up modeling, getting married –

and I had some successes along the way. I tried therapy and meditation to rise above my pain. Gradually, the spiritual part of my life became the most important to me, and I spent every penny I could make in pursuit of enlightenment. As a result, I had many deep and profound experiences.

But I'll never forget one of my most important breakthroughs regarding guilt. Even though I had done a lot of therapy and meditation, I still felt bad, unworthy and guilty, just as I had as a young child. But I had the good fortune to meet a marvelous guru, with whom I spent almost twenty years, who had helped me to navigate through these early misunderstandings.

On one of my earlier visits to the guru's ashram, I was lining up one morning for Darshan (a line of people waiting for the guru's blessing). As I stood in line, hoping to receive some form of blessing from her, I became terrified, just as I used to feel when my mother greeted me with insults at breakfast. I began to feel I was a terrible sinner who the guru would judge harshly; I feared that I might even be turfed out of the ashram. When I was next in line to greet her, I became overcome with fear, so I looked down in shame. Finally, I stepped in front of her, and she astounded me by looking clearly into my eyes with deep love and acceptance of my authentic self. She seemed truly happy to see me and welcomed me in a way that I had never been welcomed before in my life. She did not acknowledge any of my perceived sins; she only acknowledged the love in me. As I walked away, I felt a lifetime of shame and guilt was replaced with love, joy, and ecstasy.

The guru's Darshan allowed me to feel fully seen as the divine being that I am – that we all are. I imagined how it must have felt to stand before Jesus. I imagined how He would look at someone who was ill or had been accused of sin, and see through the illusion of their affliction, sin, or guilt to their true nature, their wholeness, their God-self. This was why Jesus could simply state that their sins have been forgiven.

When we look at others, we trap them with a judgment of some kind based only on what we see with our human eyes. When we see another person as just a body or personality, we are condemning them forever to sin, separation, and unworthiness. Deep inside every one of us, we feel our specialness, our connection to greatness. But most of the time, we ignore not only others' Godlike qualities, but also our own, and find fault, and focus only on the impermanent body rather than seeing beyond the form to the inherent love and perfection, which exists within all of us. We then walk around in denial of the terrible grief that arises from seeing one another as separate and feeling as if we've sinned and are stuck in this cruel world, compelled to play some role that we barely believe ourselves. We may even feel like an impostor – and that's because we are. If only unconsciously, we know that we are truly a part of God, we are divinely loved, and we have never sinned because we really are living somewhere apart from this dream we call life.

This world is an illusion – only love is true. Judgment, separation and hate are the lies that make up this world and when we are experiencing these states, we are living in the illusion that we call the world, believing it to be real. However, when we are in the states of love and oneness, these serve as lifelines propelling us beyond limited consciousness and far beyond a mere body that is capable of sinning. These lifelines can bring us back to divine presence that tells us we are still and have always been one with God, somewhat like the drop that merges into the ocean of love.

However, the game of sin and separation continues. We fight wars and kill one another because we honestly believe we're separate from that "other" over there who has done something very wrong in our estimation, and it's our job to set things right by punishing them. This is how we trap one another, by using sin and guilt, which then devolves into blame, judgment, fear, and righteous indignation, giving us many reasons that we can use to justify our attacks and to, temporarily at least, feel freed from our guilt.

As long as we continue to project onto others, we will remain in the dream of separation, which is a living hell. The only way to be free of this dream/hell is to awaken to the fact that there is only one; one being that illuminates everything, and is all love. We could bring significant change to this world by seeing through the eyes of love – seeing no sin and condemning no one and no thing.

This may seem like a tall order for a mere mortal, but we can practice seeing everyone we meet as already innocent. We can begin to dissolve the barriers that separate us. It's simply a matter of perception. Even if you dislike the person that is standing before you, stay present in the moment and perceive the person as another part of you, (which is just another part of God); a person who needs to be compassionately embraced. Then listen to what God in this form, of the other person, has to tell you. By doing this, you are taking the next step in going beyond the ego's reaction. You are learning to see through the eyes of the Divine – seeing beyond sin and judgment to our inherent purity and oneness.

I recall hearing about an East Indian saint who, whenever he would encounter someone, would silently say to himself, *"Thank you God for coming to me in this form."* He would see all others as the Divine, reflecting to him different aspects of himself and he would simply embrace and welcome them all.

As I awaken me, I awaken you.
Joe Vitale

2.6 HOW WE USE GUILT TO TRAP OURSELVES

(Looking for the Sinner)

I've heard that the souls who love us the most cause us the most suffering. My mother has been my greatest teacher. As a child, I experienced insufferable pain, and my mother inadvertently pushed me to find the truth, because the "reality" I experienced, growing up with her, was unbearable. She didn't know that, of course, but I knew this was true. One day I had moved back into the old house temporarily after my marriage ended. My mother came upstairs to my room with eyes ablaze and tears flowing. She grabbed me and cried, *"I don't know why I've been so cruel to you! I've loved you more than anyone!"*

I remember being surprised by her flaming eyes, the awareness she displayed, and the honest admission, all of which I'd never experienced in her before. While her profound lucidity did not last, this experience served to show me that I must always look beyond the form. When she said this to me, I responded, *"It's okay, Mom. You couldn't have done anything else – it was our learning together."* This made it easier for me to have compassion for her and to forgive her: I saw that she couldn't have been any other way. I was not a victim of her coarse and sometimes abusive ways, as I had once believed. Upon further contemplation, I recognized she was just a projection of something that came from inside me. Her cruelty toward me originated, in a deep unconscious part of myself. She was simply playing out aspects of myself that I hated and was simply reflecting them back onto me.

After that revelation, I made a clear decision to no longer be a victim of my childhood. I realized that the victimization I was experiencing was my inner voice or unconscious mind reporting to me what I felt about myself. Only it came through my mother's voice and her actions. Not only that, I saw how I would deliberately remain a victim in order to justify my feelings of guilt and unworthiness. I realized that I had to rid myself of the habit of making others, such as my mother, the sinner and stop projecting my own inner guilt and pain onto these innocent people who were acting as conduits for my own growth. This is the awareness we need to have to bring peace to our world.

Some scientists, (who lean toward the universe being a super-hologram), are sounding a little like the saints, who have told us that everything is pre-destined, or has already happened, (just before our brain and nervous system take ownership of it). With this realization, we can take the next step and detach more and more from the world and all of its events and dramas with amusement – free of being a victim of life or of being a victimizer of others.

The steps to realizing victim and victimizer are:

1. Your unworthiness becomes so much a part of you that you unconsciously look for someone else to feed it (as I did with my mother). This way, you can continue to feel bad and victimized, a role reversal where the victim looks for the vampire.

2. You find your "vampire" (someone who will be your victimizer), then you arrange it so they betray, abandon, and condemn you for the sins you have unconsciously carried internally. This serves to reinforce your feelings of victimization and guilt.

3. You now have your justification: "Yes, I'm a sinner – it's been verified by (whomever) so I really am bad and do deserve to suffer and therefore, feel guilty."

4. Now you can forever condemn the vampire, who has

played the role of the abuser, for judging and naming what has existed unconsciously within you. What's happened is that the vampire/abuser has acted as a channel for your unconscious guilt so that it can be seen clearly and healed. This unconscious guilt takes the form of self-hatred, fear, judgment and guilt, all of this because we believe that we've separated from our source. So the vampire's role is to merely shed light on the symptoms of the perceived separation, so we can wake up from this dream.

We look for the sinner in order to trap ourselves as well as others. In the end, we all lose because we are reinforcing the belief in separation whether we are the victim or the victimizer. The only door to freedom is to become aware of our divinity.

A simple example of this unconscious self-hate happened to my friend, with whom I used to go to the gym regularly. Each day as we walked to the gym, she would tell me, *"I'm fat, I'm too fat. I hate myself because of it!"* All I could see was a beautiful woman who was anything but fat. I tried to convince her that it just wasn't true, but unfortunately, she couldn't accept the truth.

One day, while we were lacing up our shoes for an aerobics class, a woman marched up to my friend and in a firm voice said to her, *"You are fat and you should work out more!"* I could not believe my ears. After this woman left, I asked my friend if she knew her. She was now extremely upset, answering; *"I've never before seen her in my life."* She became indignant and wanted revenge for this "out of the blue" comment.

In that instant, I remembered a gem from one of my teachers: *"You can't do something to someone that they're not already doing to themselves."* I immediately reminded my friend of her daily routine of self-judgment, but to no avail. She simply couldn't see it and angrily responded that the fat comment had nothing to do with her constant judgment of herself.

This is why and how we become victims. We think that our

outer world has nothing to do with what runs around in our unconscious minds. This example perfectly describes how we go looking for the sinner or "vampire" to play out our buried unconscious guilt or judgment.

1. As a victim, you seek out a vampire.

2. You find your vampire (in the previous example, the woman in the gym) to condemn you for the sin of self-hatred that you unconsciously carry. Doing this, you amplify the sin by bringing it into the light. This only serves to deepen your feelings of victimization and guilt.

3. Your hidden sin is now justified by this vampire's revelation. Now you can wallow in further self-loathing: "*See? Yes I'm a sinner – bad, fat, ugly, unworthy ...*" – using whatever script you've memorized to keep yourself down and victimized and endlessly guilty.

4. Finally, you turn your darkness onto your abuser and condemn them for naming and revealing what has existed inside of you for so long. You are off the hook – you can stay in your world of smallness and victimization because you now have someone apart and outside of you, a person, your "vampire," to blame for your pain and suffering.

Instead of blaming, if you could take responsibility for your pain and see that pain is merely a projection *emanating from you* rather than *happening to you*, you would see that the situation is an opportunity to practice compassion. Compassion can be achieved through forgiving this illusory "vampire." You'll then be on the road to stopping your negative self-judgments and in so doing, heal your unconscious guilt. Shed the light of forgiveness and acceptance onto your self-judgment each time it arises. In doing this, you'll see – in yourself and others – the inherent oneness and innocence of each human being, as they are simply actors in your movie, playing their part extremely well.

2.7 PUNISHMENT – THE GREAT PRESERVER OF SIN

I read a story of a man who had lied about being beaten and robbed of Oprah Winfrey tickets. He scraped his hands on the sidewalk, used a rock to make a small cut on his forehead and then told police that two suspects knocked him around before swiping his Winfrey passes.

He later admitted to officers that he made up the story because he forgot to buy the tickets and didn't want to disappoint his wife, who was hoping to attend Oprah's "Farewell Spectacular."

He didn't want his wife to be mad at him, so he said he got robbed.

All this madness to punish himself for his perceived sin and to assuage his guilt. While all he needed to do was to take full responsibility and apologize to his wife. But his fear and guilt were so strong, that he had to act out a drama instead. This is an exaggerated example of how one single person can punish themselves, by being both judge and jury and hangman. The man even ended up in jail.

We all find ways to inflict punishment on ourselves, to repent for sins that we believe we have committed. You may not realize, but many of our minor aches and pains, including our ill health are examples of self-punishment. We punish ourselves for the regretful actions we've inflicted on others, and we punish ourselves for our lack of integrity. So we feel bad and guilty and that we deserve to suffer. It's not like we are intentionally causing suffering as, metaphysically speaking, this kind of self-punishment comes from a very deep and unconscious place within us, as it's all very mysterious – in that it was all set in motion from the beginning of creation. So it's important not to judge ourselves for our illnesses but rather to see them as

reminders to love everything about ourselves and as an opportunity to turn any self-hate back to love because love is the healer.
Darshan Singh had said, *"Our soul being of the essence of God is also
love. And the way back to God is also through love."*

But instead of forgiving the pain/guilt in our mind, we punish
ourselves by projecting the pain into our bodies. And in this way,
we seem to escape from what we are really feeling and as a result,
we don't have to face the lie. That being, *"I believe that I've
separated from my Self, I believe that I've separated from these 'Others,'
and I feel bad about it."* And because we've been brought up to
believe that God is a vengeful god, we inflict punishment on
ourselves to save "Him" the bother. Hence, we end up seeking
doctors to heal our pains, thereby making the body real, hoping
for a cure for what ails us from someone or something apart from
us, whether that be a doctor, chiropractor, acupuncturist etc.
When, in fact the real healing needs to come from the level of the
mind – where the pain and guilt originated in the first place. We
need to heal from the inside out.

One such circumstance arose with a friend, who had noticed
that the pain in her back was increasing and no doctors were able
to help her. She said, *"I had a thought. Do you think that this pain
could be coming from someplace other than my body?"* Oddly, this
interaction occurred while I was writing this chapter. I replied,
"Absolutely!" As we delved beneath the layers of her emotions, we
got to a place where she admitted that in the past, there was
tremendous guilt that she had denied around having hurt and
judged a friend who had recently died. She then realized that the
pain in her body was originating from her mind.

When she realized that she was punishing herself, she experienced an emotional release. We then discussed that everything in
this world needs love. Even if we feel that we've hurt others, we
can still correct our wrong perceptions and give love to someone
even if they have passed on, thereby bringing love to ourselves.
The pain need not manifest in the body at all and we can

reconnect with the truth of who we are. Besides, if we look at this world from the holographic perspective, then time and space are irrelevant as all of us, and all of existence, are one!

Stephen Levine, author of numerous books about death and dying had started a hospice where people who were terminally ill, could go and die in dignity. While there, they would be guided through various forgiveness techniques that would help them to have completion with those in their lives with whom they still held grudges. The patients would "forgive" these others, (even if they were long dead), with the hope that they could die in peace having been able to express their angers, resentments and regrets. Then the most unexpected thing happened, many of these patients went into remission and were able to go home healed.

So by my friend owning her projection, she was able to return back to the cause – which is on the level of mind and where the love needed to go – rather than being a victim of the effect, i.e. the pain in her body. This belief in 'cause and effect' or 'karma' feeds on sin and punishment and has us spinning round and round on a never-ending wheel, hence the "wheel" of Karma. As long as we believe ourselves to be this body, there will always be sin, so at this level there is no escape, as the body is a projection of the ego. Ego is anything that sees others and self as separate. So as long as we believe in the reality of the physical body, we will constantly see separation and duality and that is all that the ego would have us do on this physical plane of existence. Hence, sin, karma and guilt will continue to prevail.

We have made what is true about us as a lie and what is a lie about us true. And then we built an entire world to demonstrate that the lie is true … the idea that life is the battleground – that is part of the lie. (10)
Ken Wapnick

And so we invest our entire life in proving that we are an illusion of limitation rather than one with God. If we could turn our attention back to the cause or source and dissolve the belief that we live only in a body, then we could rise above ego/illusion, which includes our body as the ego's projection, and we would naturally dissolve sin and guilt.

The solution is to put the brakes on the wheel of self-punishment and really examine the idea of cause and effect. But before we do that, and before we project all our guilt onto our bodies, onto others or our world, we need to look at and feel the root of this sin/punishment wheel and bring another element to it – Love, because we are so used to bringing judgment to our world and hence to everyone and everything in it. Love is the healing balm for all that ails us. Love is the revealer, the healer, the path and the goal. Without love, this world is hell.

Broadening our perspective on cause and effect is to include the idea of oneness. This in turn would dissolve the duality hence, on this level of perception; there is neither cause nor effect. On the level of duality, there appears to be an effect that follows actions because everything that we do to another is actually done to ourselves in the moment. The saints and sages of old, and now more recently, science, tell us that we are all one substance. If this is the case, then it follows that if we are all one substance, cause and effect and the idea of Time are dissolved, as it is all occurring simultaneously and according to the holographic model of the universe, there's only one thing going on, and not two. In addition, author Michael Talbot adds another slant to this, when he refers to physicist David Bohm's assertation that, *"Bohm ... still felt it was important for scientists to remember that no single cause-and-effect relationship was ever really separate from the universe as a whole."* (11)

Karma is a made up story dependent on linear time, however, actions and reactions happen together. Karma is presented in such a way that it has us walking around suffering for our perceived wrong doings and past lives (where we were separate beings in separate bodies.) These stories are relevant up to a point and on a certain level. But as we mature, we realize that the concepts we've learned are simply stories designed to make sense of this dream we call reality, which keeps us bound to the cycle of sin and punishment. But we are not really living in reality because reality means oneness with Self and Love, and which has no cause or effect. Therefore there is no karma because we are all one, and in that way, we are free from the laws of sin and punishment. Sin, guilt and punishment arise when the belief in separation arises and they dissolve when our sense of "I" ness dissolves.

Sin is relative to whomever is organizing and deciding what it is and how it should be punished. For instance, it might have been considered a sin if a Jewish person, (my ex-husband), ate pork on an important holy day. But for someone who is not inter-ested in religion, there would be no sin or punishment nor any thought of it. Similarly if my ex-husband was caught in a restaurant eating bacon and eggs on the Sabbath, he might feel guilty and a little ashamed for being caught and later might "accidentally" stub his toe and think, *"It's probably because I had bacon and eggs for breakfast."* However, if he had an interest in Hindu philosophy, he might say, *"I stubbed my toe ... must be my Karma."*

So our Jewish "friend" or anyone else for that matter has organized a whole story of sin, guilt and punishment in order to waste time in a separated state rather than resting in the still place where there is no Jewish person who eats bacon and eggs on the Sabbath, therefore, there's no sin and no punishment. If then, we drop through our illusions to that state that has no duality, the mind doesn't need to organize or make sense of the chaos of guilt and sin. Then we can see ourselves as merely actors on the stage of life.

One way that we can do this is through the act of a soul

cleansing. Let's take a moment and try a psychic soul cleanse and experience letting go into a higher frequency. We do cleanses for the body in the spring, in order to rid it of toxins that have built up over the previous months. But we rarely do cleanses of the Soul in order to rid it of toxic thoughts, labels and beliefs that have accumulated over decades, which are all at the root of all our ills. The soul cleanse is the most important cleanse of all.

Take a deep breath and rest deeply in the still place that exists – prior to any label at all. Identify all of the burdens, or judgments that you've made up, and imagine seeing them melt from you as you move into deep peace. As you cleanse yourself, a lifetime of burdens and labels can drop away and you're left with the freedom to be who you really are. This is a great way to step out of our daily movie, which can become grueling at times, and to rest our soul while returning to the deep love, which has no need for labels or organization.

Since things are dependent and dependent arising, there can be no cause and effect.
Nagarjuna

Stephen Wolinsky, a Quantum Psychologist and a teacher of Advaita-Vedanta explains this sutra by Nagarjuna in the following way. *"The substance, the cause and the effect are one. This substance is the cause and the effect also."* (12)

If we can catch ourselves before we make a meal out of the drama of sin and punishment, by remembering that there's "nothing out there" separate from us, we can save ourselves a lot of suffering. If we knew intimately, that whatever we say or do to another is said or done to ourselves, wouldn't this be a vastly different world?

2.8 THE IMPOSTER SYNDROME

The deepest split of all occurs ... for if you are to retain guilt, as the ego insists, you cannot be you. (13)

I once had a friend, and no matter what he did, or whom he interacted with, he overdid it. It was rather strange to watch, somewhat like an actor playing out a role but not very well, so it wasn't believable. Then one day I asked him, "*Why do you try so hard when talking to people?*" He looked down sheepishly and said, "*Because I feel like an impostor, and if I don't try really hard, they will find out that I really am an impostor – because I don't even believe myself. I think I must feel some guilt or something.*"

As I reflected on his response, I realized that in certain situations – I too would try extra hard to make this person that I thought myself to be, believable. I was performing; I never fully believed that I was okay as I was and I too felt that I was making everything up as I went along. I believed that if others were to find out who I really was, they would judge and hurt me somehow.

An example of this "impostor syndrome" occurred when I was in a line-up to meet with a master for the first time. When I arrived at the hall where this event was taking place, I saw people behaving in all sorts of ways as they met this master. Some were bowing, others kneeling, and still others held their hands in a prayerful pose. I tried to learn the rituals that people were performing so that when my turn came to greet this master, I would be appropriate, as while I was keen to meet with this great being, I had no interest in the outer forms. As I was approaching her chair, much to my surprise, I heard a loud voice in my head that said, "Fake!" I thought that I'd been found out. I knew that she would see that there was a split between who I portrayed myself to be and who I really am. I just wanted to make a good impression for this master, but what I felt in that moment was a terrible guilt and I realized that it was I who was attacking myself for just being me. "Why?" I wondered.

Then when I finally met this master, I was embraced with open arms. She never addressed the feelings I was experiencing, but instead she was infinitely loving. However, the split inside of me was unbearable. I thought to myself, *"What kind of impostor am I – obviously not a very good one,"* because I still felt I had been found out and exposed. Found out because even though I was drawn to meet her, another part of me wasn't all that excited as I had had direct experiences of God before without having to go through all of the pomp and circumstance, which for me was too overwhelming and was a distraction from my real self. I didn't believe rituals had anything to do with God's love.

The combination of this conflict with wanting, while at the same time not wanting, to be there was what made me feel like an impostor inside. But no matter how I framed it, all that was left was this intolerable feeling in my heart along with the guilt. This war was raging inside of me, and yet nobody around, including the master, ever said anything to me about how "bad" or "fake" I was. I was the one calling myself a fake because I felt guilty for just going through the motions of trying to fit in, when in my heart and soul I knew somewhere that I was already one with the Divine and that nothing that I did or didn't do in the world of form, could make me more or less loveable. The latter was my real self-speaking, i.e. the Self that is love. The other part of me that I was struggling to be something, i.e. the spiritual seeker that felt impure and unable to do the rituals properly, was my ego who wanted me to feel bad, guilty and a sinner. The real reason that I felt like an impostor was because I did not have the inner conviction that who I was, as I was, was already complete, whole and perfect. I doubted myself and forgot that I was already one with love, one with God.

The spiritual path wasn't the problem; my guilt that was being reflected in the mirror was the issue. Guru's act like mirrors and thus expose hidden parts of ourselves that require healing and cleansing so that we can feel our true self more intimately. So actually, this whole process with the guru was very effective because it revealed the negative programs that I had carried inside of me my whole life. I began to see that my previous 'performance' was exactly what was preventing me from aligning with my true self. Hence, I always felt a split, which led to guilt and anger. A split between my true self and the part of my ego that was telling me otherwise; and wouldn't allow me to be me. The split felt like a primordial block that kept me from knowing who I really was. I also felt that I wasn't allowed to trust the natural intuition that guides my life and knows the truth. When you are dependent upon the outer form for validation you will always be thirsty and left wanting. This thirst causes resentment and so when I was in a spiritual group, I would feel conflicted.

But when I was feeling conflicted, I was really angry with myself for pretending – or for being an impostor – for telling myself that I felt something when I didn't. When instead, all I needed to do was to let myself rest in the place of truth inside me, and be at peace. What anyone did, or whatever happened on the outside was really none of my concern. Over time, I realized that when we are guiltless, we don't need to resist anything and can enjoy any form of worship as it is all one. I saw how guilt always wants to attack and lash out at anything or anyone it sees in order to avoid the fear of being found out and punished by God for the imaginary separation. The impostor cannot exist without the ego, if one is annihilated, so is the other. So whenever you encounter the ego or the impostor, remember this, if it isn't Love – it isn't real. Then you will know who you really are – Love and release the whole made-up drama.

When we follow our deep inner knowing, life guides us naturally because we are no longer struggling against our ego and our guilt, nor do we need to feel like an impostor because we are true to the deep, solid place that knows what we need to do, and trusts in the flow of life. At the ultimate level, we are just characters in a dream, playing out our script. So when we align with the character – our true self – that knows the lines perfectly, there is no need to be an impostor and we will no longer hold ourselves outside our heart.

The real truth is, we are all impostors believing ourselves to be just this body/mind personality that is separate from others, yet knowing somewhere inside that we are something much greater. The pain of our impostor-ship is a call to return home to our divine self, and the dissolution of the split between the ego and God.

> *When we come to the world, we all drink from the waters of forgetfulness. Some drink more than others.*
> Plato

2.9 MISUSE OF POWER

The devil, guilt, sin, fear, hatred and all of the ego tendencies are symptoms of or synonymous with separation.

Everything in our life is about duality and separation. Everywhere we look and everyone we see appears to be separate from us. Most everything that we do comes from a mind that is split and separate. Consequently we feel guilty all of the time at just about everything because we can't come to terms with the fact that we feel something is wrong, wrong planet, wrong life etc. And somewhere deep inside, we feel, "What have I done wrong to find myself here ... separated from my true source?" So everything we encounter in our life, whether that be a fight with a spouse or lack of money, poor health or even the smallest irritation, propels us right back to the guilt of our perceived original separation from our true source. At times, we sense somewhere deep inside, that we are all of the same substance and are all one. But the only thing we see are the separated appearances, as a result, everybody is permeated with unconscious guilt since whatever we look at, with the limitations of the mind, is riddled with guilt and judgment – which is all our own projection.

A scientific discovery made by Aspect and Bohm found that, *"The universe itself is a projection, a hologram and that the separateness of subatomic particles is illusory."* (14) So we really are of one substance and infinitely interconnected.

A friend of mine wrote a poem on an experience he had where he saw through the eyes of love.

> *In the face of love – is the face of God*
> *When I look at you, all I see*
> *Is the face of God – in the face of love*
> JP Stevan

The mere fact that we are in a physical body means, our God self is covered over and we look at the world from our body's eyes, (separation), rather than through the eyes of God, (Oneness). This is where we unknowingly misuse our power, by choosing separation/ego over the truth/divinity. Simply put, our true power lies in the right vision.

I recall hearing a story of a Native American elder who had said, *"Inside of me there are two dogs. One is mean and evil and the other is good. They fight all of the time."* When he was asked which dog wins, he replied, *"The one I feed the most."*

In our attempt to be emotionally balanced, we try to push away guilt in favor of something more positive. This works for a while but eventually, we have to open our eyes and take a good, hard look at what is keeping us from love. Rajinder Singh, a guru of our times, likens the battle between the ego mind and the god mind to a sports team playing at home against the visiting team. Obviously, the home team has the advantage because of the support from its fans as they are playing on their home court. He goes on to describe this split mind in this way:

"When the mind is driven by its desires, it can overpower the subtle soul. One would think soul with its infinite power, could be strong and resistant, but the nature of the world is such that the mind is operating in its home territory ... the soul, is but a guest visiting temporarily. The mind has the advantage in this world of matter, whereas the soul is out of its element here." (15)

A Course in Miracles speaks about the "tiny, mad idea", where Jesus separated from God in a dream, and that God is not even aware of this dream, this world we call reality, let alone our belief in separation. Every spiritual path has some story in their scriptures describing the moment of separation. But if this illusory world originated as ACIM says from a dream, then this world that we call reality is also an extension of that same dream and therefore, an illusion. So it seems as if the true power that we are is kept down, the same power that we share with God. Because we have forgotten that we are drops of God's essence, we misuse the power of our right vision. Every day, one way or another, just by the mere fact that we are seeing each other and God as separate from us, we suffer.

Our hearts are broken from this misuse of power and separation, and we long to return to our home court. It's only through intense longing, love and forgiveness that we can begin to transcend the veils of illusion, and the wrong understandings and misperceptions that we have fashioned our lives around. In so doing, we can shed the many layers of mind, matter and illusion that cover our inherent oneness with the Divine thereby allowing us to lose our cherished individuality, though limited, and merge back into the state that is prior to consciousness.

Just sit there right now, don't do a thing, just rest. For your separation from God, from love, is the hardest work in this world.
Hafiz

2.10 THE FROZEN WORLD

Because we are all made of the one substance, if you hold even one person outside your heart, you keep everyone out, including your own self.

The Narnia series is a well-known children's story, which aptly describes the suffering of all those who were ruled by the evil witch. Everything was frozen, none of her subjects, who were talking animals, were happy. They lived in fear and even some of the kindest subjects would go against their inner standard and carry out harmful actions to appease the evil witch while under her controlling rule. Similarly, we too have the wrong ruler on our throne. Just as the queen felt that she was doing what was right for her people, in her estimation, we also have given our obeisance to the wrong ruler who, like the queen is severely restricting us by having us believe that Guilt is the rightful heir to the throne. However, guilt is an impostor and has taken over the world so that it can keep us here, reliving our loveless stories that keep our hearts frozen and separated from who we really are.

We have reached a point where we feel as if we can't go on in the same way any longer as all of our past structures are beginning to strangle us. This is a correct assessment of the situation. What we are really saying is that we can't live in this hellish illusion any longer. What we have crowned king or queen in the past does not work for us anymore. We need something different. I hear these cries all of the time in my work. Our souls are tired of living the lie. Our greatest suffering is that we are not seen divinely by each other, let alone by ourselves. We have lived far too long under the grip of the wrong ruler. There comes a point when people who are repressed rise up in revolt because a part of them knows that they deserve better and are tired of the abuse.

But the revolt now is unlike any that we've seen in the past. We are called to awaken the inner warrior with the sword of great discrimination. We're in a time where we need to cut at the root of these debilitating programs that would have us believe that we are just a limited body rather than a divine being, before they have a chance to further propagate. The only way out of this frozen "inner" land is to question everything we have believed. The ruler/god that we have contrived has us feeling angry, judgmental, greedy, competitive, jealous, unworthy, critical and to top it off, guilty. We've made up a god that tells us we must pay for our sins … as we have made many mistakes. Isn't this ironic? No wonder we suffer. But if we could realize that none of this has anything to do with who we really are, because who we really are *does not live in time*, then we could see this existence as scripted by something much greater than anything that we can conceive of. Simply put, if anything is finite or impermanent, it is not real.

Knowing this, we can simply dismiss these energies and thought forms lovingly as if by blowing away dark clouds to reveal the clarity of wide-open sky. Why this seems so difficult a task to undertake, is because we believe that we are the body/personality alone. When we identify with this body alone, we are instantly separated from our real self. Once we experience separation, we are back, living in the illusion of time, where it appears that we really need to punish ourselves for having separated in the first place. And for the most part, we are unconscious that this program, of needing to punish ourselves, is even going on inside of us. The corollary to this is that once someone steps outside of "time," then they know completely who they are and that they are already one with their Source. They know that they are loved, guiltless and free from this limited human form, free from the nightmare of sin and guilt. They break the last illusion and take a quantum leap to freedom by stepping out of the "bad: dream and awaken to a world where only peace prevails."

...You are not guiltless in time but in eternity. You have "sinned" in the past, but there is no past. (The experience of) *Always, has no direction.* (16)

2.11 SO WHO IS THE GOD OF THIS WORLD?

According to Ajaib Singh Ji, author of The Ocean of Love, the god of this world has been given many names: Gnostics call him the Demi-urge; Jews call him Yahweh; Cathars call him Jahveh; Christians see him as Satan; William Blake writes about him as Urizen; Kabir a (Muslim/Sufi) saint referred to him as Kal; and there are innumerable others. However, a common thread runs through the many religions and belief systems that hold this being in such high esteem. He is considered the god of this world, the one who balances the scale of good and bad thoughts, words, and deeds. These karmic rules are fair and just in the worlds that he rules, (physical, astral and causal); an eye for an eye and a tooth for a tooth seems to make sense in a linear sort of way. This is what we understand to be karma. If we sin we will be punished, and if we do good, then we must reap the benefits. We're easily managed by this system because of our addiction to guilt, our sense of doer ship and our inherent desire to love one another.

"Since within the framework of the Rule of Law and the condition of the lower worlds we cannot avoid sin, it is true that we get exactly what we deserve according to the Law of Karma. But since the ultimate reality of the human condition is that we are children of Sat Purush (God most high), 'drops of His essence,' Kal, seen from that perspective, prevents us from realizing our full personhood and thus is monstrous and unjust. Our mind is related to Kal (God of this world) in the same way that our soul is related to Sat Purush (God of love and sinlessness)." (17)

According to the Cathars, when we die, the powers of the air surround and persecute the newly released soul, which flees into the first lodging of clay that it finds. This lodging of clay might be human or animal. The soul is then condemned to a cycle of rebirth entrapped in another physical body. By leading a good enough life, human beings, or rather their souls can win freedom from imprisonment and return to Heaven. They believe that in order to confound the devil, it is necessary to abstain from all earthly temptations and to strengthen the inner spirit by prayer.

This example about the Cathars belief in the power of living a virtuous life describes their attempt to not buy into the egotistic limitations of this world. These limitations only serve to keep us recycling ourselves into a limited form, only to live in an earthly hell separate and apart from our true home.

Many approaches agree on one thing: the fact that something exists that is trying to prevent us from leaving this illusory world and returning to live in our true home. The true masters are important in this realm because they can help us to navigate through the many obstacles and help us progress towards and ultimately reunite with our source. When we realize that we are not a separate entity but one with God, that we are love, purity, and innocence, we see that we've never been a sinner. At this point, we discover our freedom from karma as well. As the dualists would say, the god of this world – the god of all material things including the world and everything in it – has contrived to capture souls, imprison them in human bodies, and fill them with temptations, which act as a distraction from our focus on the source of freedom. The truth is we are all divine sparks imprisoned in a tunic of flesh. Thus, a part of us that is one with God has no sin and cannot be trapped in this cycle of birth and death. Our soul is the divine spark that when empowered and identified with God discovers that it is free not just from sin but from this illusory world.

In summary:

1. Guilt is an illusion that arises only when we believe our body is real. We also believe that we are the body that

performs actions, both good and bad.

2. Because we are really beings of light and love (sparks of the divine), we are inherently good. But because we are trapped in the flesh, which is prone to experiencing envy, anger, lust, greed, pride, sloth, and gluttony (the Cardinal sins), we make mistakes and stray from our true nature, which is love. As a result, we are inclined to hurt others and ourselves in various ways.

3. Because a shroud of illusion covers us and we cannot see the divinity in others or ourselves, we suffer terribly, believing outer appearances rather than seeing the divine being in everyone.

4. As a result of these misunderstandings, we make this illusory world real instead of making our divinity real. We begin a downward spiral and guilt naturally arises.

5. Because we are love in our essence, we feel guilty when we do an action, which we consider to be sinful, so we punish ourselves and sometimes punish others. The ensuing guilt keeps us continually repeating the same cycles of sin and punishment, which become an addictive behavior. Sin needs guilt or it will dissolve.

6. Karma was established as the law of the physical realm to mete out the appropriate reaction to our actions. Lord Krishna, in the Bhagavad Gita describes this concept in the following way. When we do good actions, we create good karma, these are seen as golden chains and when we do bad actions, we create bad karma and these in turn are seen as iron chains. The problem is that they are both chains that bind us to where we must experience the fruits

of our actions – both good and bad. Ideally, if we can go beyond the duality of sin and guilt we can live in a state free of karma, at one with our true God-Self.

7. Karmic law worked to create and manage our illusion of the world, but since it was fear based, it kept us away from our real selves. If we didn't have fear, we would have love, and if we had love, this illusion could not sustain itself. The god of this world would lose us all because we would not be attracted to the concepts of sin, guilt, punishment, and karma. Instead of playing this "game," we would be attracted to our purity, innocence, and rightful place, as one with our true God.

All concepts of good or bad, original sin, karma, or debt of any kind are the products of an unawakened mind that is locked into time.
(18)
Tony Parsons

PART III

THE END OF GUILT'S WORLD

3.1 WHAT WE HAVE PROJECTED ONTO GOD

Rabia Basri is one of the most well-known female Islamic saints who lived in the 8th century. One famous quote, which is attributed to her, is her answer to the question *"Do you hate Satan?"*, to which she responded, *"My love of Allah has so possessed me that no place remains for loving or hating any save Him."*

One day, she was seen running through the streets of Basra carrying a torch in one hand and a bucket of water in the other. When asked what she was doing, she said, *"I want to put out the fires of Hell, and burn down the rewards of Paradise. They block the way to God. I do not want to worship from fear of punishment or for the promise of reward, but simply for the love of God."*

She was said to be the first Sufi to introduce the idea of Divine Love and that God should be loved for God's own sake and not out of fear, which was prevalent in her era. Unfortunately, this kind of fear-based thinking is still hidden deeply within our subconscious and is then projected onto God.

Even the word God itself, at another level is just a projection onto consciousness. We try to make God into a human, who judges us as we judge ourselves. We want to turn Him into the father that we've not had. In other words, we've given God human attributes that are cast in duality – good/bad; right/wrong. We've made up a story that God is up in heaven somewhere, watching down on us like a Santa Claus who wants to know if we've been naughty or nice. We so much want a god that is a separate individual, and we want a god who sees <u>us</u> as a separate individual. We want a god who will fulfill our material and emotional needs, while also giving us spiritual experiences, provided we are good. This can bring us a certain amount of peace, but if we make God out to be a wrathful, vengeful god who keeps track of all our missteps rather than loving us unconditionally, we will never be free from guilt and fear because we are bound to make mistakes along the way.

> "I can't imagine enjoying Heaven much knowing that the vast majority of people – or even anyone – was in Hell ... that doesn't seem like Heaven to me, that just feels like Hell. So we all end up in Hell. If one of us is in Hell, and you Love, everybody's in Hell."
> Timothy Freke

I recall an awakening experience while on a meditation retreat. We were doing what are called dyads. Sitting across from a partner, you take turns asking your dyad partner, "Tell me who you are." The one asking the question would receive the answer without comment or judgment. After a set time we would change partners and this would go on from morning till night. After a couple of days of doing this process, my partner asked me, "Tell me who you are." In that moment I had a direct, enlightenment experience that cannot easily be put into words or concepts. The pressure in my head was so profound, I heard myself scream out, "Who the hell do you think I am? I'm me!" But the "Me" I spoke of was not the ego me, it was the me that was one with everything. At this point, the facilitator came up to me and asked me again, "Who are you?" I emphatically said, "I am God." But again, it wasn't the god that I knew up until then; it was the God that just is ... no Santa Claus, no right/wrong, good/bad. In this God, the person I thought I was, disappeared into a place of such immense love, a love that dissolves notions of god being a separate individual.

After having this direct experience, even the word "god" dissolved here leaving no words to describe anything. When we enter the Divine deeply and directly, we experience dissolution of all concepts and then merge with the Creator like a "thirsty" drop of water rediscovering the ocean.

The god we make up and project our dualistic thinking upon,

affirms our guilt because as long as you believe you are just an individual, you will feel guilty, afraid and abandoned – somewhat like a child who loses his parents at a mall. He runs around in circles desperately seeking his parents afraid of being abandoned and fearing he'll never find his way back home. Similarly, we too walk around equally discombobulated because we feel lost and separate from our real source/home and wonder what we have done wrong to feel so abandoned. This is the root of all of our fear in the world, whereas the God that "Just is," is love and doesn't recognize guilt, or fear or shortcomings or any other story for that matter. This God lives within you as you.

At the absolute level of reality, we are all one substance and here all duality, differentiation and guilt dissolve because we are once again back home and at peace, prior to any outward projections onto Consciousness.

People think that renunciation means to renounce the world, or wealth, or success or foods but there is only one thing that we need to renounce and that is our belief that we are separate from God. To renounce the idea of "I," "Me," or "Mine."

3.2 DECEPTION OF PERCEPTION

Argue for your limitations and sure enough they're yours.
Richard Bach

I once had a client whose daughter revealed that she thought she was gay. The mother was devastated, and her daughter was filled with shame and guilt for the criminal she felt herself to be. They even bought a book confirming all the feelings the daughter had about herself as a sprouting gay woman. Feelings of not belonging, feeling separate and guilty, so according to this book, surely she was gay. The mother recounted to me her dilemma and then I asked her, *"Have you ever had any of those feelings yourself?"* She said, *"Oh yes, all of the time!"* Then I asked her, *"Are you gay?"* With great indignation, she replied, *"No, of course not!"* I looked at her with a sideways glance, and she knew right then that she was judging her daughter and was shocked at her own defensive proclamation of innocence. She is an aware woman and then she said, *"I see how I am separating from my daughter and subtly judging her."*

I told her, *"It seems that you and your daughter have been given a wonderful opportunity to heal the separation that you are both carrying."* This rang true for her. I continued, *"Suppose there's nobody outside of you at all and what you are seeing in your daughter and her feelings is just a part of you asking to be loved and forgiven for separating from your real Self."* I also reminded her, the label that she and her daughter grabbed onto, i.e. "Gay", and made real, was a way to widen the separation from Source – a way of not dealing with the real issue that keeps the feelings of guilt and unworthiness alive. In other words, a label helps us organize our thoughts, concepts and ideas including our feelings of guilt, but it's deceptive because labels don't allow us to walk through to the real core that transcends the psychological view. Labels deceive us by trapping us in our false perception or illusion. The labels feel so solid that a person has virtually no opportunity to free him or herself up from the deception. For instance, we are taught that a label <u>is</u> the object that it describes, but a rock is not its label as the label is only a descriptive word or concept for the object, where the word simply refers to another word that refers to yet another word and so on.

The only way out of this deception and misperception is to drop into the deep love of our divinity, of our oneness with Source, and go beyond forms and labels – recognizing that labels are just costumes that we wear and we are not the costume.

One of the things that I said to my client was, *"Your daughter is not gay, she is a pure spirit, perfect and innocent, and she is a beloved child of God first. Whatever she does after that is just a worldly identity, which we all carry, has nothing to do with the Supreme Being that she already is one with."*

What we add to the 'I Am,' is what deceives us and makes us separate. Any and all of the labels that we add to this "I Am" only limit us, identify us and separate us from each other and most importantly from our true Source, and that is why we feel guilty because we think that what we are is not worthy or okay, let alone divine. Around our necks we carry nametags that say, "I am Gary; Barbara; disabled; gay; a hunk; beautiful; ugly; rich; poor" and so on and so on.

We all wear one label or another, which only deceives us by skewing our perception of ourselves as well as others in that we only see others as their label as opposed to their true essence. In turn, others also see us as the label that we've identified with and hide behind. This is akin to wearing the wrong prescription in our glasses; we essentially are blind to the truth. This is why we have wars, violence, fear, and hatred not to mention all of the ego tendencies including pride, blame and so on. Because we believe our labels, they make us objectify each other, which is the ego's way of not letting us feel the divine love that we are. Ego can be an acronym for Edging God Out, which is what the ego's purpose is, and that is of reinforcing separation in order to ensure its own survival.

Our present world is based on the deception of our perception by making the appearances real. As a result, we are unable to view life as it truly is. Stephen Wolinsky Ph.D offers one of many explanations for this misperception, "The reason the world appears to be solid is because the nervous system makes things appear that way. Moshe Feldenkrais said, 'The purpose of the nervous system is to organize chaos.' The nervous system takes the alleged chaos of emptiness and organizes it into what we see as the world and ourself. But prior to this organization, everything is emptiness. Form is condensed emptiness and there is only one substance." (19) So things are not as they seem.

During a holiday in the Bahamas, I was laying on a beautiful, multicolored blanket in the sun, under a brilliant blue sky, white sand and rhythmical lapping waves. It was an ideal dream vacation. After a while, as I lay there resting, I began to feel an undulating motion beneath and within me. I thought, "Oh my God, I'm in an earthquake!" I grabbed the blanket and sat up, only to see the sand on the beach turn into golden, pulsating molecules.

The beach was dissolving before my eyes. Then I looked down and realized that I too was dissolving. My feet and legs had become golden molecules. I wasn't frightened though, because I was still there somehow and it didn't hurt, but I was also transforming into these golden molecules. I felt very heavy as I slowly got to my feet, and walked with great effort to the ocean, but it too was changing into the same golden molecules, so I just stood there for a while, not knowing where sand stopped, and ocean began.

Everything including me became molecules of pulsating golden light. For a moment, I felt myself disappear but then very slowly, things regained their separate shapes, and I too returned to "normal," but not really ... I saw very clearly that everything is made of the same substance. Why this happened, where I fell through from the ordinary into the extraordinary was a mystery. But what I learned from this experience has never left me. I realized that I am not a solid body but rather pure consciousness as is everything else ... one substance.

We don't perceive each other as one substance, all we see is a by-product of our conditioning, and this is duality/separation. This leads to all of the divisive tendencies that lead to increased separation, rights and wrongs and ultimately violence and wars. By raising our vibration, to where we see the one pulsating consciousness, there would be no need for labels. Labels limit our potential, our ability to see the truth by having us only perceive superficially and thereby keeping us deceived and in suffering.

In other words, anywhere we judge, resist, blame, and criticize anyone or anything in our "world" we are perceiving superficially and thereby separating from the Source of our consciousness, which is oneness. Swami Muktananda explains it this way, "You are you. You can't be anything else. You are that Supreme truth. When "I" consciousness becomes attracted to other things, it becomes limited." (20) Anything we add to the "I" such as I am happy; I am sad; I am a man; I am a woman; is contracted consciousness.

Everything that we perceive in our world has a label attached to it to help us explain or understand something. It is common knowledge that our physical universe is comprised of three dimensions: length, width and depth, (height). If there only existed three dimensions, then our five senses would be sufficient in interpreting what we perceived. But when we/science discover other or higher dimensions, then our five senses fall far short and we are left adrift on a boat without a paddle.

Suffice it to say, we can't trust our senses to accurately interpret life or experiences of anything perceivable or conceivable because they are limited to the three dimensional universe. So if something were to occur on another dimension, we would in all probability "freak out" because it would be beyond our limited concepts and understandings and most certainly outside our realm of experience. We would wrongly deny its truth or existence simply because it wouldn't fit into our limited perceptions and mindsets.

I recall hearing Ram Dass describe an interaction that he had with his guru, Neem Karoli Baba, who had said to Ram Dass, "*When I look at you, all I see is Love.*" Upon hearing this, Ram Dass thought to himself, "*Is he blind? Doesn't he see my impurities and failings?*" Only after contemplating this did he realize, "Of course, where he's coming from, all he sees is Love." This love that he speaks of is the one consciousness, and we are all one substance. This is the correct perception.

You are not merely made of the same thing, you are the same thing.
One thing, unbroken. (21)

3.3 DISSOLVING THE IMPLANTS

I've spent over three quarters of my life devoted to under-standing the truth of who I am. I've lived in Ashrams, studied numerous courses, and spent time with Shamans, Gurus and teachers. I've had many direct enlightenment experiences; shape shifted, and even experienced a miraculous healing. I've endlessly studied the nature of the mind and ego, spent decades participating in spiritual practices such as Seva, chanting, meditation etc. Lived in India and whatever other destination I needed to go to in order to understand the next level of my seeking. In addition, I have facilitated groups and counseled for over thirty years, and after all of my many experiences, I've noticed that there is definitely something preventing us from seeing the light of who we truly are.

During one of the courses I was studying, created by a brilliant master, Yogeshwar Muni, that dealt with the nature of the mind and all its conditioning, (which incidentally, for me, was a very intellectual and dry topic), I came across a section that said, "*Attitudes have been fixed into your mind with great subtlety and thoroughness mostly through the use of electronic devices. Electronic devices, used to implant ideas and attitudes into a person's mind, have existed for a long time, millions of years.*" This was shocking to me at the time, and I thought that maybe they "implanted" this into the course to wake us up!

As years have passed by, I realized that we just never know what forces are trying to control us, a belief that in this day and age seems more mainstream than when I first heard it. Whether we believe electronic devices have been implanted in us or not, we need not look very far to realize that implants are alive and well in our life. By simply looking around us, it becomes quite obvious that we are being implanted all of the time, often through the use of guilt. Even a husband and wife implant one another in order to live harmoniously, though not necessarily with an electronic device. The husband may have the money and subtly implants the wife with the thought, "If you don't do what I want, I'll take your money away from you." This may never be spoken about in words, but the wife follows his wishes by agreeing and obeying. So we may implant each other to manipulate in order to get what we want, or to just get along better.

One problem with this is that in order to do this, we must take on a False Persona, a role or a state of being that isn't who we are. For instance, we put on a smiling "false" mask in order to show the world that we are okay when we might be in grief because the implant has you believing that if you express yourself genuinely, you will lose love. We are entrapped by these implants and often, even after years of various therapies, you may still not be able to figure out why you can't feel relaxed in just being yourself.

Implants are used all the time to sell products, by laying into the mind the belief that if you use this product for the skin, people will love and respect you. So after repeatedly hearing this message, it not only gets into your mind, but you might start humming the commercial's jingle and eventually buy the product. We are under a constant barrage of manipulation, from churches to governments to work, sports and families. Everything seems to be set up to keep us, as far away from our true self as possible. Because, if we were true to ourselves, if we dared to ask questions, as the Buddha had said, *"Don't believe what I say just because I said it ... ask questions, find out for yourself,"* then we would discover that we are free and uncontrollable.

If we are, "uncontrollable" and know who we truly are, then we would have no fear, we could be real – established in who we are – but this is frightening to those doing the implanting, because anyone who knows who they are, are impervious to implants! An Implant overrides your own personal choices and freedoms in your life, most people who are used to implanting and being implanted wouldn't know what to do with someone who is established in their own knowing and are totally free.

Denial is what keeps Implants in place.

If you are reading this and have a reaction, thinking, "That's ridiculous ... that can't happen," And then you return to your comfortable state of status quo/denial, well, rest assured that that thought pattern is an implant, and you've just given in to it. This denial keeps us all towing the line, in place and controllable. It ties us down to the mundane and inane effectively preventing us from awakening to our true self. This is also how animals are trained, through the use of implants so they eventually obey the instructions and demands of the owner.

Similarly, this is how we train children, for their own safety of course, to keep them away from dangers such as traffic, hot stoves and so on. Often they need to be told over and over, even spanked. Eventually, the child reaches the point where when he steps off of a curb, or is near a stove, he will inexplicably just stop or turn around. He may not even know why or what is wrong, but somewhere he knows that he'll get hurt. He now has a fixed impression in his mind that keeps him from touching a hot stove or walking into traffic.

These implants are stronger than what many therapies can deal with. Implants run so deep in our unconscious mind that no amount of rational thinking would have any effect on them. This is why we have been so possessed by sin and guilt. These implants operate on a deep, visceral level, and there is no easy way of letting them go because they involve every aspect of our being and identity.

An example might be if your boss tells you that you're not pulling your weight. Immediately, a thought arises, "I'm bad," or "I'm no good ... " to the point where it is so debilitating, that the comment – "You're not pulling your weight" has suddenly launched you into a place of deep guilt, sadness or even depression. Nothing anyone says to you can change it. You might on the surface recognize your worth, you might know that you are not really so bad and unworthy, but still deep down, you feel you are bad and you don't know why you feel that way.

When you contact an implant, very often you will have a reaction such as an experience of betrayal or resentment, which is a good sign because this is an opportunity to contact the core guilt yet again. When we become conscious of the implant we have an opportunity to work with it. Most of the time, the implant is well hidden and busy running our lives. It creates a false sense of self, bent on reinforcing our denials and has us overcompensating to keep us from feeling this core implant/program, thereby keeping it hidden. But once we see the power of the implant, we can recognize it for the illusion that it is, as nobody is essentially bad or guilty to that proportion. The immensity of the reaction is the key.

I used to tell my clients, *"If someone comes up to you and triggers your deepest problem, thank them, because you've been given a chance to see the implant in its full blown colors and you can say, "No!" to the implant. Because deep inside you recognize that it is not only something very foreign to you it is also very debilitating as well."* We can see this implant as something apart from us that has nothing to do with who we are. You will notice that after you've come face to face with one of these massive implants and recognize it for the illusion that it is, you will be able to relate to others in your world, more reasonably and maturely.

You will also find in your heart, the capacity to forgive your perpetrator even if they have betrayed you, which often happens when we hit an implant because we are actually betraying the ego's hold on us. You may actually thank your petty tyrant or implant triggerer, since they acted as the vehicle to help you uncover this insidious and debilitating implant that has been running your whole life. So in essence, the perpetrator, the victimizer, the "other" who causes you any amount of grief, is only a reflection of an aspect of you that needs to be healed and forgiven. The following is an example of just such a situation.

When I was a child, my mother used to say to me – when she became overwhelmed or upset – *"I never wanted you in the first place!"* This always stayed with me and caused me great suffering as a child because naturally, I wanted her to want me. Only much later did this become clear to me.

I had a dream that I was sent to the earth from another galaxy in a spaceship that was travelling at the speed of light. I remember feeling immense pressure as I hurtled through space. When I finally arrived, I came out of the spacecraft and approached a panel of beings, who, once they saw me; all looked very disappointed that I had arrived. They said, *"Oh, you are not what we expected ... you are not who we wanted ... but since you are here, I suppose you can stay."* I felt a distinct oppression, like a shroud, come over me, which was very unfamiliar because in this dream, the realm I had come from was a far lighter and higher frequency. I felt disappointed and devastated, because the gifts that I had brought were not wanted and I was forced to suppress them. This is how they implanted me because I believed this deep disappointment to be true and real, rather than remembering my oneness with the divine. So the belief in the wrong power left me vulnerable and able to be manipulated. Finally, at the end of the dream I recall spinning and twirling into flesh and then life here began but the implant, *"You are not wanted"* remained and haunted me.

In my life I have often hit this deep program or implant in my work and my relationships or it would just be free floating within me as a sense of horrible unworthiness, guilt and fear. I couldn't penetrate the program or see it as an illusion; instead I believed it was true, which kept it going.

As I looked back on the dream, I recognized the words, *"You are not wanted,"* as a major implant and could see how my mother could only be a reflection of this implant. When I saw this I could also see her innocence and her confusion about why she related to me in such an unusual way.

Whether or not this dream was real or I came from another planet, isn't the issue. The deep, unconscious implant uncovered in my dream was subsequently revealed through the dynamic with my mother. Her early words were identical to the words spoken by the panel in my dream. After years of re-experiencing those same negative feelings, I recognized the dream as a gift and a healing, serving as a reminder that I am not a victim. The power in the words, "You were never wanted," began to dissolve after I identified the implant/program, which I had lived with and given power to for all those years. I was clearly shown that this lifelong reflection was in fact a symptom of the original separation. Its origin was within my own mind, and had effectively separated me from my true self for as long as I could remember, because I had believed it to be real. When I recognized this, I offered it up to the divine and asked to be returned to my true home where I am always wanted and loved.

Some of the most powerful people are not necessarily the strongest, wealthiest or most beautiful, but are the ones *who know* who they are and if someone should attempt to implant them with a limiting program, they would find it amusing. They would see through the illusion of something or someone trying to take away their essential self and they certainly wouldn't agree to it nor would they resist it because they would be beyond such persuasion. We, on the other hand, are caught and bound by these programs and are easily implanted because we are either resisting or accepting them only because we don't know our own Self – who we truly are.

The bottom line to implants is, 1/ You believe that if you don't agree to them, you will never have love. 2/ If you don't know who you are, (that you are love), then you are driven by fear. So we keep this movie going, while selling our soul to the devil/ego in order to have love. But we already are love, have love, are loved and are complete just as we are. It's no accident there are innumerable movies, where someone sells their soul to the devil, but in the end the devil/ego always betrays.

The easiest way to avoid implants from others is to be like an eagle. When crows come pecking at an eagle, it doesn't fight them. The eagle simply rises higher.

Anything that surfaces in our life, that isn't love, is a lie, an illusion and a projection of unconscious guilt.

All perceivables or conceivables are to be discarded as, 'not this, not this'.

Nisargadatta Maharaj

3.4 CLEARING UP CONTRADICTION

There was a story I read of a Llama and his students who were huddled by a small fire in their monastery in the dead of winter. The building was not providing much shelter from the wind and snow and certainly offered no heat. As the fire they had huddled around to keep warm began to dwindle, the Llama stood and retrieved a wooden statue of the Lord Buddha. He then nonchalantly placed it into the fire. Aghast, the students exclaimed, *"Master, how could you do that? This is the Lord Buddha!"* With great calmness, the master replied, *"On the one hand, yes, this is the Lord Buddha. But on the other hand, it is just a block of wood ... and it is cold."*

This was an important lesson for the students.

In our spirituality, we can tend to become narrowed, not unlike a horse with blinders on, to the point where we are no longer dealing with life as it presents itself, right now – in front of us. There is so much good and bad mixed in with our understanding; we therefore, experience massive confusion. We have heard over and over that we are all one but don't understand how this translates into life. Not unlike steam and ice, in that they are both water, the same substance, only in different forms. Similarly, the outer forms that we interact with are varied in look and purpose but are still just the same one substance.

There is only one truth; we are one with the absolute reality; and with everything in existence and this never changes. However, what we think we are, namely this body, is merely a projection onto consciousness. So how can we not have confusion if we don't understand our true self? This is why we get stuck, because we don't always see the whole picture. The following story is an example of this.

Four blind men were brought to an elephant and asked to describe it. The one who touched its tail said that an elephant is like a sweeping brush. The one who touched its body said that it was like a huge wall. The one who touched the elephant's trunk said that it was like a large hose, and the one who touched its leg said that it was like the base of a tree. Though they all touched the same elephant, they each had a different perception of it, so too in our world and in our spiritual life, there are constant contradictions. Another way of looking at this is when we take a close look under a magnifying glass at one facet of a diamond, then at another and another, we see there are many beautiful facets, but when we hold the diamond out at a distance and look at it without the magnifier, all we see is just one shimmering stone.

Our perception of this world and our various attempts at trying to better ourselves, are all predicated on the limited belief in duality, i.e. right and wrong. Life "just is". In truth, we are held in love constantly and nothing that we do here affects that love. This love is eternal, and it is what we truly are. Hence, at the absolute level, guilt does not exist at all because here we are not a separate body that sins and feels guilty. However, at the relative level of the body, which is the level of the egoic mind – where there is duality/separation, then yes, we make mistakes that need correction. We experience greed, fear, lust, doubt, guilt etc. because this body projection makes it appear as if there is someone separate from us "out there". Unconsciously we wrestle with the God/mind and the Ego/mind, but in truth there are not two, only one. The Ego/mind is the illusion. As long as we see others and ourselves in a separate way, we will keep guilt and sin alive.

Seen at the surface level, our world seems to be an odd conglomeration of contradictory elements because we live in duality. But as we delve deeper into this matter, we will see that these apparent contradictions are not real as they all originate from the same power and are hence, all of the same substance, even though they all look different. In fact, the forms that we see are illusory. But when we experience truth, we see that the great ocean of consciousness is changeless even though it appears to change.

Whether the ocean is raging one minute or calm the next, in truth it is still the ocean, so too in life, nothing is separate, it is all one. The drop is not separate from the ocean. This is the reason that we are drawn to delve into spirituality – to try and make sense of these seeming contradictions. Most spiritual teachers speak incessantly of Oneness; this only begs the question, "Why then is our daily life fraught with duality, differences and separation from each other and life?"

Some of our saints and sages describe the cosmology of this separation and contradiction in the following way; as the spirit descends from its inherent oneness with the Divine or the Absolute, a layer of mind, matter and illusion enshrouds it. The first level of descension from the absolute is where it is mostly spirit with a little matter. As spirit continues its descent, the ratio of spirit to matter decreases until it is mostly matter with only a little bit of spirit; this is where we find ourselves today, at the level of the physical form.

An example to illustrate this would be of a lamp with a bright light bulb that has a thin covering placed over it. One can still see the light but its brightness is muted somewhat. Then as the spirit continues its descent, it experiences yet another layer or covering that serves to dull the light even further. These layers are added successively until the light can no longer be seen, this being the physical level. This doesn't mean that the light isn't there or that it doesn't exist; only that it is beneath all of these coverings.

These different coverings or layers are called, the physical, astral, causal and super causal and the realm of "That which is beyond all duality." In truth, these levels only exist within the illusion of separation, because ultimately there are no levels, only the Oneness. Each level also has its own unique character-istics and identifications with time and space; in addition, each realm is seen as a more perfect reflection of the preceding (lower) one. So depending on where one is resonating, there are innumerable ways and paths and truths that are unique to each person for their journey back "home." And yet even the notion of there being a journey to get back "Home" presupposes two things. First, that there is a separate "I" seeking truth or enlightenment and secondly, that there can even be a reality, (this world), which is separate and apart from God/home.

This is why there are so many contradictions. By the mere fact that we believe that we've separated from one absolute reality, having devolved, "The one became the many," so therefore it would look like there are multiple truths alongside of the one truth – that we are, will be and have always been, one with the Divine. But we are experiencing this oneness right now, whether we feel it or not.

Kirpal Singh has elucidated on this issue, "... *the spirit, in its downward descent, gets enveloped in fold upon fold of mental and material apparatus which compel it to experience life in terms of their limitations, until, no longer conscious of its own inherent nature, the soul identifies itself with their realm of time and space ...* " He goes on to say that the great sages and mystics have based their insights, " *... not on inherited learning, philosophical speculation or logical reasoning,*" but rather on direct (inner) or "ultimate" spiritual experiences otherwise referred to as *anubhava.* (22) And finally, he concludes, that these great rishis and mystics, " *... explain that seeming differences are not because of any contradiction inherent in what they say, but because men vary greatly in temperament, and what is possible for the man of a cultured and refined intelligence is impossible for the unsophisticated peasant, and vice versa.*" (23)

For this reason people seek to discover some way of becoming free of these seeming contradictions in order to find the ultimate truth. Whether you are drawn to a teacher or a group, the only way to experience the freedom that one seeks is through direct experience of your divine nature. This is why many paths offer various techniques that are designed to help one return to the truth – a truth that is already attained, already yours … the truth that you already are one with what you seek (and have never separated from). You've just forgotten because of all of these layers of mind, matter and illusion.

Because of the different levels described from the absolute on down, there are many different teachers, masters and gurus as well as different techniques that offer many approaches that will ultimately help you to traverse back upwards to the absolute level. And even so, we are all still the one substance in the midst of all the differences and the seeming contradictions.

There was a great teacher who gave a talk to his followers and afterward, they spoke with each other. One said, *"Oh did you hear? The Master was speaking to me … he spoke of the importance of renunciation answering all of my questions."* Another would say, *"Are you deaf? The teacher spoke to me because he was speaking about the importance of doing practices to still the mind."* Yet another had a different take, as he insisted that the talk was all about the importance of being a vegetarian and this addressed all of his concerns. The teacher gave one talk but everyone took from it what he or she needed based on the level of their understanding. The listeners heard only what they could grasp and what they needed to hear at that time.

The teacher would speak not just on one level but also on all of the levels, from the gross to the subtle; from the importance of physical practices to the natural identification with the highest Self.

This is not restricted to gurus or masters alone, anything that we encounter, even a movie or newspaper headline, will speak to us and we can get from it some deeper message or teaching that can be used to help us make our way back home. Oddly, even some of the people who are the greatest challenges in our life that reflect a lot of pain and angst for us, end up actually being our greatest teachers. They force us to look beyond the outer appearances, to see the real cause of the suffering, which then can free both of us from our wrong understandings, thereby returning to love.

We in turn, follow teachers and religions so we can feel love for ourselves and for others. There are many levels of under-standing and everyone has to work from where they are right now. What is important to understand is that everything, every situation, conflict or experience is evolving us back to our source, regardless of how good or bad our daily lives look.

Let's take a look at three possible ways of approaching guilt and separation. Everything that we are drawn to do is ultimately returning us to our true home/love, so each person will go about it in their own way, whatever that may look like. As love, is the true reality, everything else is illusion.

The first way is, if you believe that you are separate from others, then regular therapy, where you look at all your feelings and relate them to your childhood and how that childhood caused you to hate some person etc. could be a valuable and necessary way to make sense of it all. Here, cause and effect are real because by living in a separate world, we affirm the existence of sin and guilt, punishment, fear and so on. From this perspective, whatever therapeutic techniques you utilize, to work within the realm of separation, will have some beneficial effects and can be important to softening the harshness of your world.

The second approach sees a belief in sin, guilt, karma and reincarnation as systems that try to explain and organize the chaos of our lives on the level of the mind. This is so you can feel at peace knowing that you are a separate being with a past and hopefully a better future. In this instance, your guilt is an important player here because it can explain to you how and why you are the way you are. If, for instance, you are angry or hate someone, the reason you are suffering now, according to this system, is because you've hurt that same person in another lifetime.

So when you realize this, then forgiveness can enter in and

your heart can open as you begin to gain understanding, see their innocence and hopefully feel more love towards the person that you had issue with, whether or not it was in a previous lifetime or not. Many spiritual groups and organizations, adhering to these beliefs, offer many spiritual practices aiding in the purification of one's karma with the goal being to become free from the world of illusion. Unfortunately, there is limitation in attempting to free ourselves from illusion by using illusion, as it only keeps our story alive, but sometimes by the grace of God, illusion is dissolved, as ultimately we're not the doer of actions and enlightenment can happen anywhere, on any path at any time.

These first two are based in duality and by our seeing that there is another "out there", separate from ourselves. However, they are both positive in that they are making strides towards realizing the oneness or the similarities between others and ourselves.

The third way is primarily for those who wish to experience their oneness with others, and who are questioning their beliefs in separation. The result from trying this technique may be a little more immediate. Again, if we are faced with someone with whom we are angry and are having difficulty seeing our oneness with them, then simply asking yourself this question could transform our experience dramatically.

First, though, we need to recognize that there is, "no one out there," that is separate from us, and that all that we see with our physical eyes, is simply a reflection showing us aspects of ourselves that we either hate or love. Then ask yourself, "What part of me is this person reflecting?" At this point, we need to realize that whatever is in our world, is us and if we hate or harm another, we are only hating and harming ourselves, and anytime you deprive someone of love, you are also withholding that love from yourself.

We have to want to experience the truth and to be willing to ask for help from our higher Self. Seeing through the eyes of the Divine is to see the Truth as it is. Then we must be ready, or at least willing, to have our "separate" self dissolve, through transcendental forgiveness. A simple affirmation, as you look into the eyes of this other, might be: *"You are pure spirit and you are whole and complete as you are."* Speak this from your heart and then see their innocence as well as your own.

Another simple technique that I have found useful is to say, *"Thank you for taking what I would not have myself."* This is an indirect way of bringing peace to the ego-based separation. Understandably we respond to others as we do, because that other person really looks like they are "over there," apart from us, doing something we find fault with and are not able to see within ourselves. But if we can look deeply within, we can discover that we too have similar tendencies. In fact, in our darkest moments we should see that there's nothing that happens in the world, that we have not already watched moving through our own consciousness. This is why instead of condemning others as sinners; we thank them for carrying the burden of our own denials to show us our ego. We all contribute to everything that happens and the pressure and pain of separation has to be released in some way, so some innocent soul is used as a mirror for this release of the unconscious guilt.

That is why we need scapegoats, like criminals, politicians or movie stars, so we can project our unconscious guilt onto them so we no longer have to carry it ourselves. In order to turn this around, we need to see Innocence and in order to see Innocence; we must turn the projection back to our self. This can be humbling, for in so doing, we take full responsibility for what we see and begin to recognize that there is only One consciousness, not two. In this way, you will glimpse not only another's innocence but also your own, while melting back into the Divine.

Then finally, if we see this life as a dream, which is a projection onto consciousness, we see that we are merely players in a movie and just like an actor, we are simply following the script.

This life is just a play and we the actors in it ...
William Shakespeare

At this stage we are better able to understand that we are of one substance. We have no need to see people or things as separate from ourselves, and it is here all striving and doer-ship dissolves because we have a better sense of who we are and what animates us. In other words, when we finally surrender ourselves back to the god-self or beginning, we realize we have never done any of these actions. They just happen through us as they are scripted to unfold. This is the real freedom that we seek.

So in our life, we are always going through expansions and contractions. These seeming contradictions are part of the play and may make no sense to others, but nonetheless, are perfect in their orchestration. Any philosophy student knows that just because an argument is logically valid, that is, the conclusion follows deductively from the premise; this does not mean that the conclusion is true. Similarly, no matter how spiritually evolved someone may be, they still need to cook food, shower, clean house and use the toilet. (So different actions or behaviors are needed at different times.)

Evolved souls are just ordinary people, who have a gift and powers that they've been graced with, but we tend to project qualities that are unrealistic onto these beings and yet if they seemingly make a mistake, then they are completely invalidated. We have difficulty uniting our divinity with our humanity. The whole point is not to be caught by the form or logic of things; this is how truly free beings live, in the world but not of it and their ways are often mysterious to us.

This is why guilt loses its power because it can't organize that which is illusion because guilt is part of the illusion and hence, not the great balancer of good and bad deeds as we've been led to believe.

Instead of seeing guilt as angst or suffering, open up your vision to instead see guilt as a reminder to call home and then return home. Eventually the way will open up for a reuniting with the Divine. Then over time, our ideas of separation will lose their solidity, then our seemingly contradictory life will become more real and there will be less need to pretend and worry about how the form plays out. The contradictions we perceive can be seen as the dancing play of consciousness, in a world that has the appearance of separation and duality.

In a holographic universe, even time and space could no longer be viewed as fundamentals, because concepts such as location break down in a universe in which nothing is truly separate from anything else. (24)
Michael Talbot

3.5 THE END OF THE WORLD

The experience of time disappears along with the world, much like the ending of a dream.
Nisargadatta Maharaj

There are so many movies and television shows that depict the end of the world through catastrophic events. When 2012 was approaching, many were convinced that it would be the final destruction and the end of our world, as we know it. But the saints and sages tell us that the world we perceive arises and subsides with our consciousness. From this perspective, nothing has ever happened at all. In other words, there is no world outside of us, so how can something without a beginning have an end?

I remember hearing a devotee ask his guru, "*Is the world going to end?*" The guru replied, "*No, because people have not finished up their Karma yet and they still need a home to do that in.*" So as long as we are still believing in separation, cause and effect, sin, guilt and punishment, we'll need a world where we can play it out, until we finish this off for good. Until we can look at the world – our own world, and see that it has always been a dream and that we have never been separate from Source or Love and that no one exists in separation from us, this world will remain intact.

If we could see that every tiny thing we interact with, whether that is a person or a plant resides within us and is one with us, then our need for a world in which to play out all of our dualistic notions would come to an end. This would be the end of Karma, because we would know that we are the cause of and not at the effect of life. The scientists also tell us that at the quantum level, cause and the effect are both made of the same substance so they are one and the same.

So armed with this understanding, there would be no one to

fight against, no one to project upon or be victimized by, as we would see all as One and the same.

When we understand that we are not real and solid but simply projections onto nothing and that we have never left our Source, then what need would we have for a world? Imagine a blank screen upon which a film is projected – the action, characters and events seem real, but we know they are not. The only difference between the screen characters and ourselves is that we think we are real, but we too are a projected manifestation of nothing. Ramana Maharshi was a great teacher of this concept, (being) – "*You are not.*" I heard of one example of a student who travelled a great distance in the 1940s just to see Ramana Maharshi. When he finally arrived, he fell at his feet and begged him, "*Show me who I am.*" To which Ramana Maharshi proclaimed, "*Go back the way you came.*" (25) His other students, sitting nearby were shocked. But he explained to them later that what he was really saying was to trace the "I" thought, back to before it arose.

In the book, *You Are Not* by Stephen Wolinsky, he refers to Alfred Korzybski, a Polish scientist, who explains this idea of the, "end of the world" from a scientific perspective. He says that the nervous system and the brain organize and form the representation called "I" by forming a veil that is made of consciousness, which made the "I" believe it is, but which ultimately is not.

The "I," which "you" imagine that "you" are appears after an experience has already occurred. Hence, before the "I" appears, YOU ARE NOT. (26)

Both Wolinsky and Korzybski's work helps us to understand why we are illusory. When we realize this world, that we think we see, is not actually there, then our only job is to go back from where we came and forgive and dissolve our projections thereby turning the nightmares of sin and guilt back to eternal love and oneness.

Every time we love, we end our world because love dissolves illusion.

When not one thought of sin remains, the world is over. It will not be destroyed nor attacked nor even touched. It will merely cease to seem to be. (27)

A Course in Miracles

3.6 QUANTUM FORGIVENESS
(The Leap to Freedom)

Yet time waits upon forgiveness that the things of time may disappear because they have no use. (28)
A Course in Miracles

Only Quantum Forgiveness can heal Quantum Guilt by collapsing time.

Every religion, every spiritual group and anything that points to upliftment of mankind alludes to the importance of forgiveness, but what does that really mean and what or whom are we forgiving?

Generally, if we have done something wrong or have hurt someone in some way, we are encouraged/advised to ask for forgiveness from that individual. We might say, *"Please forgive me for acting out of line"* or *"... for saying something hurtful."* This seems helpful, to a point, but does it really work? Can we really forgive another's "body" with our "body?"

In a world of separation/duality, when we forgive another person for a perceived injustice, we are actually separating from them even more by putting our attention on their guilt or transgression rather than on their innocence and oneness. In fact, we hold our self as separate from or better than them because we perceive the wrong action that they had committed, as coming from them and not originating from us. In other words, true forgiveness can only come out of oneness and not separation. It is ourselves that we are forgiving for projecting onto another our unconscious guilt. In essence, the "other" is ultimately innocent.

In the comic strip from 1971, Pogo summed this up simply when he said, *"We have met the enemy and he is us."*

This is why all the world summits to stop war and conflict are not as successful as they could be because they come together as an "Us" and "Them" model, rather than from the perspective of "we are all part of the One" model, where we are all responsible for this shared experience of guilt and blame that we've placed/projected onto each other. To recognize that, *whenever you see a problem, you're always there* is a great way to begin forgiving projections because it serves as a reminder that there's nothing "out there" that is separate from us and we're only seeing it because it's coming from within us.

Taking responsibility for what we see in our world is to see the world as "us" because it is we who see it and it is from us that this world springs. This does not mean that we see ourselves as being the "doer" of everything, thereby reinforcing the guilt that would naturally follow; but rather, seeing what's already there within us, that is naturally unfolding in front of us for the sole purpose of bringing compassion and love to all of creation.

It is from this place that our inner work with forgiveness can begin. From a very early age, we have perceived everyone in our life, as existing outside of ourselves. We have been conditioned to objectify, judge and separate ourselves from others in order to establish and emphasize our uniqueness. This kind of thinking only serves to reinforce the duality that this world is predicated on. The highest forgiveness teaches us how to perceive the "outer" world as simply an extension of ourselves; aspects of ourselves that we are often unaware even exist. This type of perception is upside down to how we've been conditioned to view the world, and yet it is the most important reframing that we could do.

Just as in meditation, one turns one's gaze within and whatever images arise are seen simply as whiffs of clouds passing by – not to be grabbed or focused on – as they are just projections from the mind. This same approach can be used in an "Open-eyed" meditation, (our day-to-day life) whereby we perceive everything in our world as a projection of the mind not to be grabbed or focused on. But what we see can be used to identify where we get caught in the illusion or Maya.

In reversing our learned perception we can see this world as purely a projection coming from us, then we can transform all of our relationships with others as well as with ourselves. To paraphrase Gary Renard, the author of *Disappearance of the Universe*, he says, *this world is happening by us and not to us.* Essentially saying that we are not victims.

When you think of forgiveness, think of the world that you see along with everything in it. This is your world because you are the one who perceives it. If you are the perceiver, then you can take back the projections that create the world that you see. Not unlike sitting in a movie theater, once the film is over and the projector is turned off, you remember that the images you saw on the screen never really existed except on the screen. In so doing, this immediately eliminates the idea of sin, guilt, and blame that you've placed on others and on all manifestations of "us" over here and "them" over there, in other words, separation. If the entire world were the ocean and only the ocean, one could not say that a wave separated from the ocean, because it's all ocean. Similarly, if we could remember that this world is just a dream and everything and everybody in our world/dream is made up of the same substance; our belief in separation would naturally dissolve.

Regardless of whether we consider ourselves spiritual/ religious or don't care at all for anything remotely spiritual, know it or not, we are on a journey back to where we came from. And where is that? For now, let's just call it love. The bottom line here is that there are only two reasons for doing anything in the world, first is to give love and the second, to receive love. Boiled down, whatever you do is either an attempt to give or receive love. What is so special about love? Love is our true home and everything else is the illusion.

The practice of forgiveness is actually meant to bring us back to love, not a personal love, but an impersonal love, otherwise known as universal love. Universal love does not contain attachment or possessiveness as in personal love. Universal love is alive and flows with the energy of consciousness. We can experience this by emptying the vessel, which is our own self, so that we may receive the constant flowing of love from the Divine. As it is, our vessel is full of ego, concepts and beliefs, and so there's no room for anything else.

The way to empty the vessel in order to receive the love that is our birthright is through forgiveness. However, the highest form of forgiveness is to forgive the illusion of ego and separation out of existence. It is not about forgiving another person, where we might feel better than them, or feel sorry for them, as is usually the case. This only reinforces the belief in duality, the "us" and "them" mentality. But rather, in recognizing that whatever is going on with another is <u>also going on within us</u> and they are just the mirror reflecting back to us, ourselves. What we are forgiving is the reflection, or as Psychologist and teacher of the ancient Hawaiian practice of forgiveness Dr. Hew Len calls it, "The data."

The purpose of this cleaning/forgiveness is to erase the data that presents itself to us in the form of others by taking complete responsibility for what we perceive. "Their" problem is really "Our" problem. Just as looking into the mirror and seeing your hair is mussed up, you can't change what you see by reaching into the mirror; instead, you must take your hand back to yourself and change yourself first and only then will the reflection change.

We are dissolving the covers or veils that hide the light that we all are as one. When we forgive, we are not forgiving people, but rather dissolving the "data" the covers/veils that only serve to keep us separate from who we are. The body itself is one of the biggest veils that we identify with, and so our forgiveness would be to forgive the belief in being this body alone, and be reminded that we are one with the Eternal, one with Source. Then slowly we realize that this body that we all identify with, has nothing to do with who we really are. Then we see the one pure being looking through our eyes at Itself.

Forgiveness at this level is helping us, and all "others," to collapse time and return "home," to the great ocean of Love. This way we are reuniting with the source of all love, bliss and freedom. Freedom from hate, blame, guilt, sin, pain and suffering to name only a few. Time collapses when we truly forgive – by seeing innocence where blame and guilt used to be. The undoing of time occurs, as it is no longer necessary because it is time's job to keep the illusion of separation in place. Then we can move into time-less-ness where fear, guilt and separation are no more. So forgiveness is not only a messenger of love, but also a vehicle to return to love.

When we see through the illusion by forgiving the projections we've placed on our world and the people in our life, we collapse time. It can be seen as a speeding up or shortening of our karma. In east Indian spirituality, the practice of pure satsang is similar because it is said that when one attends a satsang, and sits in the presence of great love or perhaps a great being and ones complete attention is on the divine, for a good period of time, one can feel a massive cleanse of delusion and projection, thereby removing the idea of separation and shortening time.

A friend shared an example of this shortening of time, in a day-to-day situation, with me. She was constantly berated by her employer and had become terrified to go into work. She spent a period of time of practicing true forgiveness, where she took complete responsibility for everything and everyone in her world, including the abusive employer. When she reached a point where she no longer blamed him or feared him and could see the innocence and purity in him – beyond the appearances – he changed radically. After this time of her forgiveness practice, when she arrived at work, he said to her, for the very first in all her years there, "Good morning sweetheart," with a big smile. Needless to say, she was shocked but knew why this transformation had taken place.

By her forgiveness practices, she took a step closer to a world of light where the darkness of sin and guilt could no longer cast its shadow. She was cleansed of some of her unconscious guilt. Her outer reflection changed and a bad situation now reflected her purity and innocence rather than her fear and guilt and time collapsed because she no longer needed to have those negative reflections plague her over and over again.

Take a moment now and practice seeing through the eyes of a master or mystic. Think of an experience you've had when someone triggered you by reflecting back to you a veil or program that upset you. Our initial reaction is to distance ourselves from that person, objectify them, blame or criticize them. But remember that they are you and you have come together so that a cleansing or healing – through forgiveness – can occur. Always see yourself as the originator since what you have perceived is in your world. In this way, whatever you have projected onto another cannot remain, and all they are left with is their innocence and by doing this, you take a leap to freedom.

Forgiveness can be used to see the innocence of everything in our world, even a little rat. A friend of mine had trouble with a rat that had taken up residence in her house. She was horrified, couldn't sleep and felt trapped by this little creature scurrying about her living space. She called me, quite beside herself, and shared with me her experience and upset. I immediately acknowledged that this rat was also in my world, just by the mere fact that I was hearing about it. So I told her that some deep program of separation is asking to be forgiven for all three of us, including the rat!

I then asked her to look at what feelings the rat was bringing up in her. She said that she felt trapped. I asked her, "How are you similar to this rat?" or rather, "What part of you is this rat?" She responded with, "*I feel trapped by the rat and I guess I'm feeling trapped in my own life too.*" After a brief hesitation, she continued, "*Oh, the little rat feels trapped too and just wants to get out!*" Here, she saw the rat's innocence.

I too resonated with that trapped feeling in my own life so together, she and I did a 'forgiveness', where we said to our Higher Selves, "*I'm sorry, I forgot that I am never trapped when I am with you Great Spirit. I only feel trapped and afraid when I'm in my ego/mind.*" Then we just sent love and blessings to the rat for mirroring our own projection. Within minutes, this rat found its hole again and returned "home." Then my friend plugged up the hole never to see the rat again. We both felt that a miracle had taken place.

Eternity is one time, its only dimension being always. (29)
Gary Renard

3.7 RIGHT USE OF POWER

The weak can never forgive.
Forgiveness is the attribute of the strong.
Mahatma Gandhi

We can't even fathom the great power that exists inside of us when it is turned towards the light. When we understand the immensity of this power that we carry in our hearts and minds, we will never feel powerless again because we will see the strength that lies in the true love, which is our right use of power.

Real forgiveness is a human's highest power as it can dissolve separation. To witness the power of forgiving from a place where we are joined as one mind is so amazing. The most difficult, but life transforming part of forgiveness is the ability to forgive those in our life who have hurt us deeply and who we have cut away "forever." Because when we push even one person outside of our heart, we push out everyone, as we are all one.

In my experience, forgiving my mother was the hardest thing I ever did. I met with so much resistance and rage inside that I felt forgiving her wasn't possible – nor did I feel that she deserved my love. And yet, I persisted even though it took a long time, because I knew that we are here to leave our world in a more uplifted place than when we arrived. These "karmic" contracts that we have with others, while difficult, if used properly, can free us from the strangle hold of hatred, guilt and judgment that only serve to ruin our own lives.

I would spend every day while I walked thinking of my mother and saying silently, *"Please forgive me. I love you."* As I repeated this mantra, that was suited to the situation at the time, I noticed that I resented having to even do this forgiveness. I felt angry with her all over again every time I tried it. Sometimes I would even telephone her and try to feel something positive like compassion. She would often criticize me or tell me how much potential I used to have, "*Too bad you failed by making all the wrong choices.*"

This would propel me back to my anger again, and I would get off the phone feeling hurt and sad. But, nonetheless, I persisted. Then one day, while doing my forgiveness mantra again, I saw a flash of light and a snippet of an image of my mother and I. In the image my mother and I, though we stood next to each other, were still distant. Along with this vision, came the words, "*You need to get closer to true forgiveness ... you're not close enough.*"

It took me a week or two to understand what this very strong message was telling me. On the day that I saw the deeper significance of my previous message, which was guiding me closer to the truth, I called her only to receive the usual denigrating comments, but this time, I felt more anger than I could imagine and was ready to give up trying to forgive her. All of a sudden, I realized what I had been teaching others for years, "*There is nobody 'out there.' Nobody can do anything to you that you're not already doing to yourself.*" I hated hearing my own words, but if I wanted to be authentic, and walk my talk, I needed to listen.

So I took some time and I looked at all my anger, resentment and unmentionable thoughts that arose within me, but this time I removed Mom's image from my mind. I realized that the anger and resentment had existed within me for as long as I could remember. I also saw how much I projected onto my mom, because it looked like what she did and said to me was the cause of my anger, so I blamed her, thus leaving me free to feel victimized and to create an identity that shaped my whole life, but never allowed me to be happy. In a sense, it was my karma because she was just a projection of my pain and guilt. And it was only my karma because I still saw her as separate from me so I believed that I was a victim or at the effect of her actions.

Prior to this, I was seeing her as the cause and I was at the effect of or victimized by her. As a result, my life was always a struggle and reflected all of the limitations that came out of her mouth, as judgments directed at me. When in fact, they were coming from me and I needed her to help me to become free from this horrible self-deprecating program. She unknowingly did this by showing me – regularly – what was inside of me, not unlike a channel of the darkness. I saw that I needed to break this cycle by stepping out of it and to forgive not her, (as I was beginning to see her innocence in all of this), but to forgive the program itself that we both shared.

This would free her as well, from the contract that we made at some previous time. Armed with this insight, I began praying, *"Please forgive me, I forgot, I am already one with you Great Spirit. I've been caught in illusion and projected it all onto my mother and have therefore been creating war in this world rather than love."* I really saw how those closest to us, have the job of showing us our "data"/programs that we've believed to be true. They show us this so that we can get free, not so that we should suffer and hate one another. Perhaps my mother wasn't the kind of mother that television portrays, but the gift she gave me was of the highest love, because I was forced to evolve myself in ways that would be liberating for me as well as others.

The experience with my mother helped me to better understand karma. For example, one day I was feeling tremendous fear and a really uncomfortable feeling in my body and mind as well as feeling angry at my surroundings, including everyone that happened to walk by me. I recognized that something was wrong but I didn't know what it was in the moment. I asked for guidance from my higher self, *"Please help me to see the truth here."* I was subsequently shown that I was experiencing extreme fear and guilt for even having the fear.

When I recognized what was wrong, I was relieved somewhat. I spoke to Spirit and asked, *"Please help me heal this guilt and fear that I'm experiencing."* I saw that I was projecting this fear outward, to distance myself from it, because a part of me believed that I could lessen the pain that it brought me by doing this.

Quite naturally and effortlessly, I returned to the cause and felt the fear deeply. I then prayed, *"Please return me to where there is only love."* Shortly thereafter my whole body relaxed, my world looked brighter and I felt that I had been cleansed from the karma that I was experiencing in that moment. This could have turned into a nightmare had I not taken full responsibility for this feeling and had instead continued to make the anger real and attack someone with my words or actions ... this is also how wars begin and that is how we create and are subject to karma.

When we have unconscious guilt arise, (which may come in the form of guilt, fear, anger or any separating thought form), we project it outward and so you have an effect. Karma is about <u>not</u> taking responsibility for what arises in ourselves and <u>not</u> cleaning it up at the root. Because karma is cause and effect, and if we go back to the cause, and make a correction, then the effect dissolves, and in that way we dissolve karma. For instance, if I had been able to catch my wrong understandings with my mom, that created a mess that traced through my whole life early on – 1/ I would have constantly forgiven this separation that came up in me. 2/ Not projected my pain onto my mom. 3/ Saw her innocence.

Had I had the correct understanding earlier in my life, I would have seen my mother's judgments as illusion and continued loving her regardless of what came out her mouth. I'm not suggesting that anyone take abuse from others, and should this be the case, to do what is necessary to take care of yourself, which might be to take space. However, the forgiveness should never cease, as you are only forgiving the programs that emanate from you, and because we are all one, you are not just erasing your own program but this is also affecting the whole that manifests as your world.

The significant point here is that all of this is the unconscious, metaphysical guilt – which is the belief that we have the ability to separate from the source of love or God. And so because we believe that we've made this choice, we all feel guilty and so we project all of our guilt/pain onto others. In this way, we believe that we don't have to take responsibility, because we've mistakenly believed we've released the pressure by blaming another. The karma here is that we suffer for our actions towards self and others, and rightly so, because we are one and the same. But we don't need to play it out, if we can return to and bring love to the cause before it can create a negative effect.

We all have someone in our life, a father, a sister, an ex, a boss, a neighbor or a child; all of these "others" are there to show us – Us, and our job is to catch the mess early. And to clean it up by forgiving, not the other person but the program or unconscious guilt, which is just something that arose in us from the original separation – a separation that never occurred.

We have never separated from anything; we are simply in a dream and will one day wake up and return to the love that has always been with us – as us – for eternity. This is our greatest contradiction. On one hand we are one with the Divine, sinless, while on the other hand we have all of these beliefs and programs that stand in our way of love. Forgiveness is the highest game you could play in this movie that we are starring in, because if forgiveness is approached earnestly, it has the ability to dissolve time, illusion – separation itself. Then we get to taste the fruits from our right use of power.

I think that if God forgives us we must forgive ourselves. Otherwise, it is almost like setting up ourselves as a higher tribunal than Him.
C.S. Lewis

PART IV

RETURN TO INNOCENCE

4.1 MAY THE FORCE BE WITH YOU

The Force that brought you here knows every action the body needs to take and will see to it that it takes those actions.
Ramana Maharshi

This is where Quantum Physics and the ancient sages meet. Quantum Physics can now show us that when a thought arises it takes a split second for the brain to react, and for the mind/ego to then take possession of the thought and say, *"It is my thought."* So the thought arises when the Quantum wave collapses. According to Ramesh Balsekar, he refers to Brain Surgeon, Benjamin Libet as having said, "A personal awareness of that choice comes about one half second later than a readiness potential that appears in the brain wave," and Ramesh continues, *"Thus there can be no free will."* (30)

Another philosopher and 18th century scientist, David Hume said, *"Because of the delay in how the nervous system works, the self only sees what has already occurred."* Many scientists in the field concur with these findings. This theory in itself eliminates the guilt program ... or any program for that matter, as we are not the doer of actions, as we have believed.

An East Indian Mystic, Nisargadatta Maharaj takes it a step further and says, *"When enlightenment dawns, you will realize that you were never born, nor have you carried out any worldly actions."* (31)

In Buddhism, one of the Nirvana Sutra's say, *"I am not the doer."* (32)

Scientifically speaking, another reason we are not the doer of actions is because nothing exists but consciousness, so everything is made up of the same substance, which means everything happens simultaneously as one. So there is no separate "I" trying to be something. This oneness eliminates the "I did it," belief and subsequently the guilt that always follows.

Spiritual practice is an attempt to reform or transform a non-existent self or subject I. (33)

These spiritual and scientific truths reveal to us that we are not really here doing anything, so how can ego/guilt even exist? Our essence is already with our Source and has never been separate.

Most people are perplexed and wonder how they can bring this teaching into their life, the teaching that life itself is illusory and a dream. If we believe this dream to be real, we make it real; it's like actors in a movie forgetting that they are actors and believing themselves to be the characters they are playing even after the filming stops.

But like the actors who know who they are, we too have only to remember that we are not one with these names or personalities that we have identified with and are playing out as actors. It would also serve us to recognize that we do nothing of our own volition. At this point, when we really deeply understand this, we can rest, in what Ramana Maharshi had said when he referred to the Force knowing every action that needs to be taken and will see to it that it takes those actions.

This is where true peace begins, not unlike sitting in the back seat of a luxurious Rolls Royce that is being driven by an expert chauffeur. As you sit there enjoying the ride, you can feel all of the burdens and the guilt that you've been carrying for eons dissolving. You will stop worrying, you will trust again while feeling free from your own neurotic perfectionism. Your striving and struggling will drop away and whatever actions you do will arise naturally and without any struggle. You won't be attached to the results, and you will see these actions unfolding effortlessly. You will make a better spouse, parent, child, worker, employer and friend. Hate will be non-existent, compassion will grow and you will rest in this great Force, finally free from the dream and of the laws that chain you because you will no longer believe yourself to be limited to this body. You will realize your limitless-ness. Your inspiration will flow, no longer blocked by these limiting programs and identifications. So we'll actually be, "In the world but not of it," and we will be carried on the wave of the great Force forever.

4.2 RETURN TO ONENESS

Most spiritual books refer to our oneness. Even people who are not remotely interested in spirituality have heard about the concept of oneness – the idea that there is no separation between us and other beings. Oneness is a great concept, but how does it relate to our everyday lives?

How can we look, act and think so differently and yet be one with everyone else, especially with those who cause us distress?

According to the poet saint, Jalaluddin Rumi, "(The belief in) *Separation is intended to create such an acute intensity of longing, that the soul experiences great ecstasy upon the final return to God.*"

We seem to be living with separation everyday, but are we really? Not according to geneticist, Dr. Aaron Shafer of Stanford University. He tells us that, "*The DNA sequence in your genes is on average 99.9% identical to that of any other human being.*" (34) (And within a family, it is 99.95% identical). Therefore only .1% of our DNA is responsible for all of the differences that we see in the world and in the people around us.

We have Quantum Physics, enlightened beings, and even geneticists confirming this ancient truth that we are essentially all of the same substance. So whether we love or hate each other we are for the most part one. In other words, we really are all one family as the pop songs tell us. So what has gone awry? All these "others" are family yet the world is filled with divisiveness, objectification and conflict.

For centuries, the great spiritual leaders have exhorted us to accept our oneness with God and with each other. Unfortunately, we have been unable to do this because this world focuses solely on the .1%. And since our attention focuses on our differences, we naturally judge, compete with, compare to and fear what we don't know or can't understand. This ultimately leads to some form of conflict and potentially an all-out war – from a relatively mild argument with a friend to a full-on attack on another country. This .1% separation is the reflection of the belief that we have separated from our Divine Self. Attack comes from original Guilt because we attack the idea of separation, thinking relief will come, but it never does.

Focusing on differences and projecting guilt onto others is like cutting off your nose to spite your face. Projections increase our feelings of separation, when all we really want is to connect with others or feel the oneness/love. Feeling separate from our source and others makes us sad, depressed, anxious and frustrated, which can lead us to various addictions. We search for something to take the pressure off of the multitude of emotions that arise, such as our anger, fear and guilt, because we are out of touch with the 99.9% that we share with all human beings. We really suffer because of our obsession with the .1% and yet, somewhere deep inside, we know that we are all one family. And when we are separated from a family member we feel pain and guilt, no matter how we cut it.

This shows that love is stronger than fear because the desire to be one with others will not leave us alone. J. Rumi says, "*Suffering is just the soul's longing for God.*" So when we grow tired of being only the .1%, and want to return to the 99.9%, we trade in the few pennies that are meted out sparingly in exchange for the infinite wealth that awaits us, then we can pull ourselves out of the muck and the mire of all of our dramas. To do this, we start by seeing each other as one and the same as ourselves. Hence, the people that we hate or judge are actually directing us to transcend separation.

Always ask, "*How am I similar?*" In that way, we will be looking at a world that is one with us because what we perceive "out there" is simply our own projection. We are looking at our own reflection in the people and situations that we encounter. Thus, anything that we hate in others, we see only because it exists within us, as do those things that we love in others.

When we look at others without projection, oneness ceases to be just a concept. Our life becomes one of unconditioned love for self, others and all of life. By remembering that every bit of separation we observe is only part of the .1% of the whole, then all negative experiences are simply reminders to turn our attention to that which is infinite. We can use the power of oneness to create a world of love, in place of a world of guilt and fear.

Play the game of separation and oneness like a passionate lover of Truth. Endeavour to reconnect with love and Oneness with the same longing that you have for any worldly pleasure, and waste no more precious time being tricked by the limitations of the .1%.

There is only one soul – which is our unlimited oneness
as spirit. (35)

4.3 SEEING THROUGH THE EYES OF THE DIVINE

A few years back, I read an article in the newspaper about an elderly couple that was celebrating the wife's 100th birthday. In the accompanying picture, they were both quite wrinkled and bent and she was in a wheelchair. The husband exclaimed to all of his guests, "Look at her, isn't she the most beautiful woman in the world?" He was worshipping her and staring into her eyes, but in truth, he was worshipping the divine in her. Obviously, she was no young beauty, but he was seeing beyond the outer form, and was responding to the brilliance of the divine self within her that also resides in each and every one of us.

When we see another, from the divine and expanded state of consciousness, we are often awestruck by their tremendous beauty and immense love. If all we saw was the divine consciousness in others, very quickly the form would dissolve and the pure essence would emerge. Imagine what this would do for our relationships, our marriages, and our countries. Unfortunately, we are often hard pressed to be openhearted, and struggle much of the time to even smile at another, let alone be able to see others in their divine and expanded state of consciousness. This divine state is not unlike the aliens in the movie, Cocoon, when they took off their earthly body, a body of pure light was all that remained.

Generally, the way that we are taught to view this world, which includes all of our beliefs, is really rather ordinary and limited as it is cloaked in separation. So when we look upon another person, we see them through the eyes of the physical body alone, which naturally leads to judgments of others based solely on how they look, act, what their status in the world is or even how they might be able to benefit us. In essence, we are seeing these divine beings through the eyes of guilt – our own guilt and judgment that we carry within us from our belief in original separation from source. In believing this lie, as A Course In Miracles says, we believe that we are powerful enough to actually separate from God, which is absurd, and as a result, we feel that we are "bad" and therefore project our self-judgments and guilt onto others.

There is a false covering that distorts our perception and tells us that we are not one with God; this is simply wrong understanding. This would be like looking into the face of a beautiful baby and then judging them for being too small or too round or too cute! And yet, most of the time, we can't judge a baby because their purity, innocence and the godliness of a newborn is so very evident. We too are like those babies, in that if we look inside – beyond the form – we see the soft and fragile beings that have been so hurt by years of coarseness from these wrong understandings existing within both ourselves and others. So of course, this has impeded our journey on the road back home to the truth.

Sometimes, in the most unexpected moment – Grace offers us a glimpse of pure vision allowing us to see through the eyes of the divine. The following story is such a glimpse.

I was living in an ashram, and every day I had to ride on a bus to get to the main building. On one particular day, I was feeling intense irritation. It was the middle of summer on the east coast, and it was hot and humid and the bus was packed with people. They were all swaying back and forth with the bus's movements. A mantra was playing on the speaker system, droning over and over. It was becoming unbearable to me. I felt separate from everyone and I felt an irritation and a pressure building beyond belief. I was on the verge of bursting. The bus continued to bump me around in this muggy space until I reached the point where I was ready to rip the speakers and the mantra from the walls! But somewhere I knew better, so instead, I pleaded and prayed, *"Please help me remember who I am ... I can't bear the separation and hatred any longer."*

Almost immediately, something shifted and the pressure and irritation ceased and in just a split second was replaced with a wave of love. We all disappeared and became one being swaying in bliss, and held in absolute love. I felt I was swimming in nectar. At this point, I even loved the sound of the mantra! All this took place in a matter of a few seconds.

This feeling stayed with me for quite a while. As I walked around, everything I looked upon – every fallen leaf, every pebble, everything that existed, I saw as one and the same, as Divine love. After that experience, I knew absolutely, that nothing exists but love and that we really are all made of the same substance. And this divine love is constant and unchangeable, regardless of the form it takes. After this, when I would look into another's eyes, all I would see was divine love gazing back at me.

We can make a shift from living an ordinary life to living an extraordinary one by finding out <u>who</u> is living this life – in other words, "Who Am I?" Why our life is so ordinary, dull and filled with conflict is because the ego is calling the shots. When we see from the ordinary, we see people as separate. We see them through our physical eyes alone and therefore judge others according to how they look, act – in essence we are seeing others as separate and are seeing the outer appearances of our world only.

This is the ego's world, though there is another perspective that we can align ourselves with that would give us an extraordinary experience of this life. Swami Muktananda describes the one who really lives this life in this way, *"You are you. You can't be anything else. You are that Supreme truth. When "I" consciousness becomes attracted to other things, it becomes limited."* Anything that we add to the "I" such as, "I am a man; I am a woman; I am wealthy or poor," is contracted consciousness and a projection of our unconscious guilt because everything we see appears apart from us.

So to continually identify ourselves with our true nature, which is Supreme consciousness, is to begin living our life in an extraordinary way. That very situation that causes us difficulty, that person and that problem can be the reflection we use to return home, to feel the divinity that we really are. By seeing past the false appearances, we can begin to return to the stillness that exists before our outer physical manifestations even arise.

Sometimes a heartfelt prayer is most effective. In your prayer ask for the guilt and feelings of separation to be removed. We can humble ourselves in our helplessness, and look into the eyes of another without labels, guilt or judgment and to fearlessly feel and see through the eyes of divinity that only knows the words, "I Love You."

Spirit cannot be seen with any instrumentation of this world. It can be seen only with our spiritual vision. (36)

4.4 THE HIGHEST SERVICE

Everyone wants to be valuable in their world and useful to their fellow man or society. And so, many have stepped up to help the children, the elderly and others in need, as well as doing whatever they can to improve the environment. Some people give money, others give of their time, some offer their physical strength while yet others give their mental brilliance or computer skills. Then we have the movie stars and the poets, singers and dancers who uplift our spirits and our hearts with their gifts.

But the very highest service is often unseen and not very well understood. In fact, an individual who does this unseen and unpaid service may even seem lazy to most. The form of their service may not be seen as valuable based solely on what society values, which often has nothing to do with what matters to the soul or the heart.

Oneness is difficult to understand, because what is generally encouraged and sought after is to establish our uniqueness and "specialness." Our differences are applauded and rewarded while our oneness is discounted and even ignored. So we are all desperately seeking attention by trying to be different from each other and yet, in so doing, we become uncannily similar... same body, same hair, same lips, same breasts, same car, same attitudes – you get the picture.

This constant striving to be different serves as a reinforcement of an "us" and "them" mentality and perpetuates the delusion that we are an island unto ourselves. Taken to the extreme, this leads to excesses that ultimately deplete our world of resources, food and water. Our basic needs are jeopardized because everyone wants to be different by having three or four homes, four or five cars, and hundreds of shoes and on and on. Our planet can't sustain such waste that stems from over consumption by a fragile ego that seeks to be different yet in so doing is no different from anyone else.

If we only knew what good could be created from forgiving the belief of separation, beginning with ourselves, then our love alone could radically change our perceived world for the better. As we would cease looking outside of ourselves for fulfillment and instead begin looking within ourselves – to tap into the infinite ocean of love and bliss that lies in wait for our return. Then we could never return to our old life consisting of attitudes such as objectifying, judging, blaming and punishing.

An example of a higher service, that could go unnoticed, might be discovered in something as simple as being angry with your child. You can go one of two ways, you can continue to project your unconscious guilt by blaming and punishing the child or you can catch yourself by remembering that you are one with this child who is simply mirroring aspects that exist within yourself – that you don't like to admit to.

When we see that the problem originated within yourself and that the anger was there before the child even acted out, then we can see the child's innocence. Once you recognize this, then it is easy to see that the feeling you are experiencing is coming from within and not as a result of anything that your child, or anyone else for that matter, is doing. In that moment you could make a plea to your higher self, God, Source, Universe, whatever – *"Please forgive me, I forgot that I am not separate from you and this child (or other), and that we are made of the same substance, totally loved, whole and innocent. We are one spirit and I love you. Show me what I need to embrace or forgive about myself."* This is one form of supplication that you might wish to use.

On occasion, I would have a client come for a session with their uncontrollable, screaming child. I would simply ignore the screaming, because I knew that the origin of this was coming from the parent – and not the child, provided the child was not crying because he or she was in pain or ill. As soon as we identified what the mother was "unhappy with" and "screaming about" inside herself, miraculously, the child would immediately calm down.

So when we choose the "high road" or higher service, we begin to live our life from the inside rather than outside ourselves as we've learned. Five ways to live from the high road are:

- Recognize the negative patterns that have dictated how we've treated others.
- We stop projecting blame and judgment, by attacking others with our thoughts, words and actions in an effort to assuage our feelings of guilt and separation.
- We consciously choose to forgive the separation – forgetfulness, judgment of this "other" because we see that the problem exists within us and not within them, in fact they are truly innocent.
- We invoke our Source, God, Spirit, Allah, Jesus, Buddha whomever or whatever represents infinite love to us.
- We then join together as one spirit, innocent and whole and return to our oneness with Love itself.

The highest service is often unseen, unheard and selfless. Great teachers can bring a group of people together and take them to deep peace, without saying a word. They know so completely that by aligning themselves with their true self, they will profoundly affect all who have gathered ... even if it's in the tens of thousands. We too have the same potential with everyone in our own life, because by remembering that no matter what another person is doing they are our family, our world. The way we can best serve them is by remembering that there's no one "out there" but our own God-Self.

So with that understanding, we too can bring great peace to those we come in contact with. The only thing that you can truly give another is your inner state. For instance, if you are with someone who is angry and agitated, you'll feel that person's agitation as well, whereas, if you are with someone who is peaceful, calm and loving, you will also feel that way, even days later!

What we don't realize is that when we forgive the belief in separation, with the help of Spirit, we can affect our whole world, as we are entangled with one another more than we realize. Our forgiveness could result with one less starving child because they may find food. Someone somewhere may choose to walk away rather than harm another in some remote part of the world because of your forgiveness. A genius may come up with an idea that may heal a deadly disease, or a war may stop or a sick person may become well. An addict may heal, and somewhere a closed heart might open for the first time. Even a threatening storm may subside ... This is the highest service that may go unnoticed by most but could have far reaching effects on humanity. This would bring our whole world to oneness because within every particle lives the One that we are and that we are joined with forever.

In quantum physics, there is a central principle known as quantum entanglement, which seems to support the idea of our inherent oneness. In very simplistic terms, quantum entanglement occurs when two or more particles interact and their wave functions become entangled. So they now have properties that are dependent on each other. If something were to happen to one, then instantly, the other particle, regardless of distance – across the room or across the galaxy – would also be affected. Quantum entanglement seems to point to a true oneness within the universe.

Children who are born twins seem to exhibit such interconnectedness also. But a specific example of this idea of oneness was described in a news story about two wild herds of South African elephants that lived in the vast Thula Thula game reserve. Because they were unpredictable and violent, they were destined to be shot as pests. However, a conservationist,

Lawrence Anthony, who was known as an "Elephant Whisperer," intervened and rehabilitated them thereby essentially saving their lives.

Many years later, on March 7th, both herds, that lived in distant parts of the reserve, began a solemn, almost funeral like procession, (which took over twelve hours to complete), to Anthony's home where he had died on that date. They remained for two days, "paying their respects," and then returned to their homes. In the article, these words by Rabbi Leila Gal Berner, Ph.D., beautifully sums up our oneness with everything.

"If there ever were a time, when we can truly sense the wondrous 'interconnectedness of all beings,' it is when we reflect on the elephants of Thula Thula. A man's heart stops, and hundreds of elephants' hearts are grieving. This man's oh-so-abundantly loving heart offered healing to these elephants, and now, they came to pay loving homage to their friend." (37)

We might not know what is affected as we open our heart to forgiveness, but things will be deeply affected. Most of what exists in the unconscious mind we will never figure out thus leaving a very small percentage of the mind that we can claim to understand and work with. But we can't claim the fruits of our forgiveness; we just do it for the sake of love. So your mission, should you decide to accept it, is to continue to implement this higher way of seeing all of life, that is, seeing every person as a part of you, as one with you. The only way to affect our outer world is by continually identifying with our own greatness! Because we've been asleep, we've forgotten and don't recognize that we carry the power of God/healing within us.

Identifying ourselves as divine is where true humility comes in because when we know that we are not the doer of anything, especially healing, then we can open ourselves deeply and naturally thereby allowing the love and forgiveness to go to where it is most needed.

The beauty is that anyone can do this. You don't have to be

mature, wise or strong – you can be young, frail or innocent. Anyone at all who is willing to forgive the illusion of their world can positively affect others clear across the globe. You can be lying alone in a hospital bed nearing death or be a small child on a school bus. Simply saying, "I love you," to all those in your world, (especially those whom you are upset with), can have profound and far reaching effects and blessings on strangers even on another continent – just as their prayers can have an equally profound effect on you.

The only thing that affects and dissolves separation is seeing through the eyes of Divine Love and forgiveness. I recall a Shaman in New Mexico being asked, "What can I do to help heal Mother Earth?" The Shaman replied, "Don't worry about Mother Earth ... heal yourself first."

Many may have heard of Ram Dass and his great work with getting the word out about the heart of spirituality, feeding the hungry as well as his tremendous work with death and dying and later with Aids patients. In one of his talks, he reflected on how he was travelling extensively to teach and speak to multitudes about love and spirit, but he wondered whether his friend, who was meditating for the world in a cave in the Himalayan Mountains, was really accomplishing anything. But after reflection, he realized that his friend was having as much of an effect on the world as he was with all of his travels and speaking engagements. Ultimately, there was no difference. It is in allowing life to be, and by not forcing anything that we align with the great force, which is the greatest service to humanity that we could possibly do.

To see a world in a grain of Sand
And a Heaven in a Wild Flower,
Hold Infinity in the palm of your hand
And Eternity in an hour.
William Blake

4.5 THE PERFECT RELATIONSHIP

"The greatest suffering in the human form is that we are not seen as already perfect and divine."

I've spoken with many people, with diverse backgrounds and from different cultures, who feel that they can no longer bear the conflict and pressure in their relationships. Such complaints are reflected in our divorce rates, which are unprecedented, and they beg the question, "What is the real purpose of relationships?" Many people are recognizing that relationships based on externals such as sex or power or just not wanting to be alone are like houses built on shifting sand. They won't hold up when the waves and the storms come. The delirium of romance can be intoxicating, but once the honeymoon stage has passed, unless we deepen our connection to the real essence of Union, we will only flit to other conquests, never experiencing the deep rewards arising from relationships based on True Love.

The turmoil of personal relationships is exacerbated by stress arising from the acceleration of time and the proliferation of technology, and is reflected in the violence and wars in the world, and in the destruction of our planet. There are so many creative ways to describe the belief in the separation from source that we experience. The Hindu scriptures speak about this age as Kali Yuga – the dark age of man, or the age of quarrel and confusion.

At such a time, all of our ego tendencies are amplified, which is problematic on the one hand, but also poses a unique opportunity for our souls to reunite with the Oversoul or God more rapidly than they would otherwise. Just as coal, when subjected to intense heat and pressure, can become a diamond, the human being, subjected to the intensity of Kali Yuga, can become one with the God Self, which is the true source of relationships. Unconscious guilt can be healed in personal, intimate relationships faster than anywhere else, as our deepest separations arise when we are face to face with love.

Our soul work starts with the ones we love, the ones who know our deepest secrets and our worst fears. These close relationships are the primary stepping-stones to learning how to love unconditionally. But bringing love and compassion to one another in these dark times is more easily said than done. So often our insecurities, disappointments, or expectations – stemming from our belief that the other person is responsible for our happiness, can get in the way. No wonder we want to run from or push away the relationships that most strongly reflect our darkness. It's our erroneous belief that they are the cause of our malaise, when in fact they are merely reflecting back to us only that, which exists within us already!

Just as Kali Yuga is an opportunity for the individual soul to remember itself, it is also an opportunity for our relationships to evolve as we learn to embrace one another and to have compassion for the human foibles that we all share. Those who have been in long-term relationships know the rage, hatred, and disconnection that can arise as we mirror each other's deepest pain – unconscious guilt. How can we bridge such separation? How can we become one with those we love, whether they are partners, family members, or co-workers? How can we transcend the endless conflicts about finances, domestic routines, and intimacy issues, never mind the cultural, religious and political disagreements that create even more reasons for us to push one another out of our hearts? Communicating our feelings about these things may not necessarily help, if they are not shared in an openhearted way, or if the other is not ready to hear what we have to say.

Perhaps we can take our cue from the great 13th century mystical poet, Jalaluddin Rumi, who said: *"Wherever you stand, be the soul of that place."* This applies to our hearts as well as our physical surroundings. It expresses the "Perfect" relationship to others and to Life itself. When we can be the soul of the relationship that we are in, when we can remember that this person whom we might be upset with just wants to be seen through the eyes of Love, we can change the lens through which we are looking, and instead of seeing only the daily problems and accompanying flaws in the other, we can see their inherent innocence and divinity and our oneness with them.

We can often shift out of our dissatisfactions in relationships when we focus on what we are grateful for rather than on what is lacking. When we focus on our complaints, we will reinforce others' shortcomings, but when we focus on love, gratitude, and forgiveness, then we empower the other. This applies not only to our personal relationships but to our world as well.

Another practice that helps transcend blame and hatred in relationships is to ask ourselves this question: *"What part of me is he or she expressing right now?"* This is an effective way to own the deficiencies that we so often project onto others. Not one of us is free from darkness. This contemplation can help us develop compassion and love for the other because it reminds us of our own foibles. When we keep even one person out of our heart, we keep out everyone, including ourselves.

I had heard a talk by the scientist, Gregg Braden, author of *The Divine Matrix*, who spent twelve years deciphering a code embedded in the cells of all life forms. He discovered that the elements of our DNA are linked to letters that form the words, *"God eternal within the body."* This astonishing find means that all living beings are purported to be intentionally coded in the same way with the same message, and are a part of one another and all of life.

If we as a species were truly able to embrace the power of this decoding and what it says about our true nature, we would be eternally at peace. The gurus and masters have known this for centuries and have constantly been reminding us that God exists in every living being. Up until now, we have given this message purely a religious connotation, which has often created more division than harmony. But perhaps this scientific revelation can cross religious boundaries and inspire us to transcend what separates us, to look beyond the outer form of partners, families, friends, communities, cultures and planet, and see the deep truth that God dwells within every living being.

We can treat our Earth as a part of God and together we can honor the Source of all life and expand this relationship to every realm. Focusing on the Love of God that abides within us helps us see the God in others. We can be the soul, or the love, of every relationship that we engage in. If enough people had the courage to set their ego aside, put others first, and back down from power struggles, we would create a chain reaction that would transform our world. The words of Sakyong Mipham Rinpoche, a Buddhist Lama, can serve as our guide: *"When you're happy, I'm happy. That's the formula. First you, then me. That's all happiness is."* (38)

Where there is Love there is no ego. When we make our love stronger than our greed, we will be able to protect each other as well as our Earth. When we make our love stronger than our judgments, we will listen to and understand the unique beauty and intelligence in others. When we make our love stronger than our pride, we will see God in everyone, even our enemies. When we make our love stronger than our criticism, we won't sweat the small stuff. When we make our love stronger than our doubt, we will never feel alone. We will have a constant relationship with the Perfect One, who knows our every thought, word and deed, and is closer to us than our own breath. Every day, we will see the whole world and each person in it as a part of us and we will experience the sheer joy of being in the most Perfect Relationship of all.

As long as the sun and the moon exist: no one but your own self
is at the heart of your joy.
Swami Muktananda

4.6 TRUE SELF-WORTH

Many years ago, even after a decade of intense spiritual practices, I could not seem to rid myself of a deep unworthiness that permeated my being. Unworthiness lurked beneath the surface of my day-to-day life, taking the form of doubt, incompleteness, sadness, and of course, guilt. The unworthiness was bigger than me and many of the techniques I tried were like placing a small Band-Aid over a large wound.

I would watch others, who were very positive people, attempt to rid themselves of their troublesome feelings by getting a new hairdo, buying a new car, taking a course or going into therapy. Others would attend transformational workshops and come away from these events feeling significantly higher and more alive than before. And they would invariably bring home positive affirmations, designed to make changes in their outer life. Others would become addicted to the "High," the euphoria and keep going back to the next workshop in order to get their "Fix."

While all of these undertakings produced some wonderful experiences, many of the people who attended these uplifting, life affirming workshops, did not realize the benefits are short lived. The reason why they are short lived is because often the core issue isn't being looked at or addressed. Over time, our resolve to continue with these various self-help techniques and workshops fade as we slowly slip back into self-doubt and the lingering sense of "*I am not good enough*," despite all of our efforts.

I was fed up with New Age Band-Aids and fed up with persistent feelings of unworthiness. So I decided to travel to India to ask my Guru directly to please remove my unworthiness and guilt – miraculous things can occur when we receive the blessings of a great being. After a grueling twenty-two hour trip, I arrived in the ashram exhausted but determined to have my unworthiness removed. The next day, I lined up for Darshan, (where visitors are able to meet with the guru in person and receive a blessing).

When I was finally in front of her, I was afraid. But I looked deeply into her eyes and asked her, *"Please remove this unworthiness and guilt from me."* She looked at me in a strange way, and I was quite shocked by what I saw in front of me. There was a thick covering that prevented me from connecting with her in the way I wanted to. A thick Plexiglas barrier seemed to be separating us and there were multicolored prisms of light emanating from the guru and it looked to me as if she was directing them at the barrier. Then everything became surreal and seemed to unfold in slow motion. She was showing me what was in the way of me experiencing my true self-worth. This experience was not cut and dried, but rather mystical and complex ... something that needed to be deeply contemplated.

As I turned to leave, a wave of deep guilt and profound unworthiness washed over me and I almost fainted. Gurus sometimes are like Homeopathic remedies in that their grace acts to amplify whatever is going on for a short time – better known as a healing crises – and it doesn't all happen overnight. It may take years to become evident that change has taken place.

Over the years, my sense of worthiness did strengthen but it wasn't the 'worth' of the ego, with all of its outer accomplishments. What I received was a deep knowing that I am truly loved and absolutely innocent. I no longer needed to believe any of the spiritual or worldly shoulds if those beliefs did not support the real truth, being that we are already perfect and absolutely loved. I also realized that spiritual practices are only there to keep our minds focused towards truth while helping to remove the veils that keep us blinded to this truth. This is a question and answer between a Zen master and his disciple:

Is there anything that I can do to make myself enlightened?

As little as you can do to make the sun rise in the morning.

Then of what use are the special exercises that you prescribe?

To make sure that you are not asleep when the sun begins to rise.
(39)

I remember watching the baptism of a baby when I was a child. I asked my mom, *"Why do they put water on the baby's head?"* and she replied, *"So it will be cleansed of its original sin. We are all born unworthy and with sin."* Even then at that young age I wondered, *"How could a beautiful little baby be sinful and unworthy?"* The memory of this never left me.

For years, I thought that such beliefs were just part of my Catholic upbringing. However, years later while I was studying East Indian scriptures, I came across the concept of "Mala," which, I was surprised to discover, is very similar to the Catholic notion of original sin. In this belief system, human beings are limited by three Malas, which are like coverings over the soul. "Anava" is the original Mala, which gives rise to the other two – Mayiya Mala, which creates a sense of duality and worry about what others think of you, (this felt like the Plexiglas covering that the guru was working on earlier), and Karma Mala, which makes us act from ego and helplessness. Anava Mala maintains that we are separate from God, and are therefore incomplete and unworthy. It's as if we have been implanted with insecurities, low self-esteem and unworthiness in order to remain separate from the Love that exists within all of us.

Yes we have veils over our soul but the veils are just that, veils, they can't define us as we are created by something so much more evolved than words or doctrines. While cloaked in these limited beliefs, how can anyone become free while at the mercy of these Malas? The best way to deal with a Mala is by facing it head on and admitting our vulnerability instead of projecting the unconscious guilt and unworthiness outward onto someone else. We can then forgive our misunderstandings and bring ourselves back to the love that we really are.

I saw one example of how Malas operate when I recently read about a study of women who look at images in fashion magazines. The study revealed that 99% of these women judge themselves unworthy. I am sure that men are similarly triggered by corresponding messages, as are people in our culture who seem "to have it all." So why is our sense of worthiness so fragile? Why is our true worth so hard to access?

Meister Eckhart, a great 14th century Christian mystic, wrote: *"God expects but one thing of you and that is that you should come out of yourself in so far as you are a created being; and let God be God in you."*

To *"let God be God in you,"* requires deep humility and trust. When we are in a state of humility, we know that we are a part of something much greater than our ego self; but when we are experiencing unworthiness, we are identifying with our ego alone. For so long, we have derived our identity exclusively from our body, mind, and senses. Deep down, we are haunted by a sense of impermanence, especially as we age. With such a limited identity we can't help but feel unworthy.

True worth and true permanence arise from identifying not with our external form or circumstances but with the Creator of all things. The only way out of the illusion of unworthiness is to dive into our deepest Self, into the pool of Love that is our true birthright. It is time for us all to be baptized again with the waters of our True Nature, which has never been impure or lacking.

We are all actors in our own movie. We have all been given a great gift that can help us in every situation. This gift is our human life, which is filled to the brim with Love. As in every movie, there are obstacles that make our story interesting. Our antagonists are those people or events that try to make us forget that we are beings of light and love. As heroes or heroines of our own movie, we can dig deeply within ourselves to find that strength and power that is always there for us. Then, when the darkness of doubt and unworthiness arises, we will be able to declare, *"No! I am worthy because I am part of God."*

Let this declaration of worthiness be your magical mantra. Repeat it any time that you feel the shroud of negativity or limitation arising, and watch the illusion dissolve.

Be the hero of your own movie. Know your own greatness. Pour the water of renewal and remembrance on yourself, and on everyone and everything in your world. *"Let God be God in you."*

"Oh traveller! Seek the path that lies within you. You and your Beloved are in the same body. Your Beloved is pervading everywhere but not being perceived ..."
Maharshi Mehi

4.7 THANK YOU

Every day of our lives, we exchange energy with another person in some form or another, whether it be the waitress, the bank clerk, the gas station attendant, our partner, our kids or our colleagues. In all of these interactions we probably say the words, "Thank you" at least a dozen times a day. But have we ever taken the time to really understand the essence of the words, "Thank you?"

Who are we really thanking? Are these just empty words we've learned from our parents or society, to be said only when someone gives us something that we want, or is there a hidden secret locked within these very words? In our busy lives we usually stay on the surface with our interactions because our unconscious guilt doesn't allow us the time to dive more deeply within.

Lurking just below the superficial appearances lays the true wealth and love that our hearts and souls are longing for. I discovered this secret doorway many years ago when I was coming out of a deep meditation. I just happened to glance at my hand and something strange happened. I couldn't stop looking at this hand, as if seeing it for the very first time, I thought to myself, *"I could never create this hand on my own ... something/ someone created me."* All sense of myself, as the doer of actions and thoughts, dissolved.

I was awestruck in that moment because I suddenly and mysteriously realized that my hand was the gift of love. These hands that I had up until that experience, taken for granted, revealed the truth. I couldn't believe my eyes, as I looked in amazement at how every tendon, bone and muscle moved in the most perfect way, and how every finger was designed to pluck the many notes of this life, and to allow me to give and receive the music of love that this life offered. I could not stop saying,

"Thank you, thank you, thank you," to the source of this life.

I saw that the true secret of life is that we already are love, but it is hidden from us by the mind's constant focus on the outer forms. Everything we need is already within us.

It struck me how blessed we all are just to be alive. This experience unlocked a door to a world of infinite love within me. I recognized that the abundance and love that we are seeking outside of our selves would never fulfill us for very long. But the love that is available to us from the Source or the Creator, cannot be surpassed by anything of this world, and is filled with infinitely more riches than we could ever imagine.

I also realized that if I could only look more deeply beyond the superficial appearances, I would invariably find this love waiting for me to turn my gaze its way. It would be available regardless of what I had been feeling or thinking, just as the sun's ray makes no distinction on where it shines.

With this new understanding, I began to see others differently. I saw it was the source of all life that was in fact giving love to me through others and that same source was giving love back to others through me. I began to understand what oneness really is. And if we actually knew how perfect we already are, we could not judge or hurt others or ourselves because it is the same one power that flows through and animates each one of us. I heard a saint once say that it's not how much we've manifested, it's how much we've loved that makes our lives meaningful and rich. With this understanding we could stop the war that we are all fighting both inside and out.

When the power of love overcomes the love of power, the world
will know peace.
Jimi Hendrix

Imagine if you would, a world where we could feel true gratitude as we received the service from the waitress. Imagine if we could look beyond the appearance of another and see the very source of their life, **even if they don't know or see it themselves.** We could look into their eyes and silently say, "Thank you" to their eternal self. So every bank clerk, partner, friend, politician, gas station attendant etc. would become yet another opportunity to say thank you to the Source of all life. Once we know the secret of true gratitude, we would realize that no one needs to be changed or "fixed," they need only to be loved and thanked. And if we all could practice this secret, in just one moment, we could turn our world from one of conflict to one of fearless and guiltless divine love.

How can I thank you
When the ever-blooming garden of your creation
Is a manifestation of one continuous thank you.
(Excerpt from *The Magic Doorway into the Divine*) (40)

4.8 HEALING ORIGINAL SIN

All creatures have been drawn from nothingness and that is why
their origin is nothingness.
Meister Eckhart

How can we heal something that has never existed? How can something that is outside of God even be? Because everything that we perceive or conceive of is an illusion, nothing separate can exist! The definition for illusion in the dictionary is, "An image or representation believed to be real in our mind's eyes, but is not actually real." Similarly, the concepts of sin and guilt are not even relevant as they are just words – concepts, which are made up and therefore amount to nothing!

When I was a child, I somehow picked up a word, F_ _ _. So I began innocently repeating it as it was a new word that had no meaning for me, but everyone else around me squirmed every time I would sing it repeatedly. They would be in shock and horror trying everything to get me to stop. But it meant nothing to me and I couldn't understand why they were so uptight about a stupid four-letter word. In my innocence as a young child, I saw the illusion and power of our concepts and the meaning and importance that we place on syllables.

So in a sense, our world can be seen as an outward, made-up projection coming from us. If we didn't project outwardly, there would be no story of a beginning or an end … this world would not be.

In the Bhagavad Gita, Lord Krishna says, (to Arjuna), *"You can commit no sin, nor can you do a meritorious deed. Your original under-standing is clouded by ignorance. That is why you think in terms of sin and merit."*

The great teachers and scientists tell us that our origin is made of nothing, so how could there be sin and guilt for how can "nothing" sin? Furthermore, we are also told that everything is pre-determined. Someone asked Ramana Maharshi, "*If I take this fan and place it on the ground, is that action pre-determined?*" Ramana Maharshi replied, "*Certainly, every single action is pre-determined – every second.*"

There have been innumerable references to this world being, "A movie." A movie is a continuous stream of parts, but the parts on their own wouldn't make any sense. And the whole movie we call life, is already completed and is simply playing itself out, much like a movie in a theater. We sit there and watch a movie that has already been finished – in other words, the movie is not happening in, "real time."

This brings into question the common held belief that we are the creators or "doers" of our actions. Yet scientists are now concurring that actions happen first, and then a half second later, our brain registers the thought wherein the mind/ego takes possession of it and claims that they were the originator of the action. We've experienced the feeling of this half-second delay when we've had a déjà vu.

One such study entitled, "The Electrophysiology of Intuition," showed that the heart responds before the brain would respond to outside stimuli. The test subjects were wired up to record the functioning of their brain, heart and the inter-action of the two in "response" to random pictures that were presented on a computer screen. These pictures ranged from pleasant scenes, like flowers to frightening pictures that would illicit fearful reactions. The test subject's body actually responded before the picture was even displayed. The heart responded first, then it would send a signal to the brain, its response was then followed by the body's reaction, which occurred as the image showed up on the screen, and only then could the test subject become consciously aware of it. "*It appears that the heart and the brain (later) have access to a field of information that is not bound by time and space.*" (41)

I really resonate with this material because I've experienced it time and time again. For example, for years, every Thursday evening, I would get together with two friends to take a long walk and then attend a spiritual discourse, which included a video talk by a popular guru. While on our walk we would regularly have a deep and heartfelt discussion and sharing about one topic or another and many of our discussions were quite profound.

Then when we went to the discourse, we were quite shocked and surprised when we heard the video talk (that we had never seen before), as the teacher would invariably say, virtually word for word, the same observations and conclusions on the same topic that we had discussed on our walk earlier. At first it felt like a big coincidence, but it became commonplace to us as it seemed to happen every single time. We realized that somewhere we knew what was going to be said or happen before it actually took place, a sort of Déjà vu.

Then I came across another more commonly recognized incidence, especially to dog owners, of something quite similar. Dr. Rupert Sheldrake, who is widely recognized for his theories on Morphic Resonance, (42) had conducted a series of experiments that measured a dog's propensity to anticipate and "welcome" the arrival of its owner, often ten minutes before they even arrived and while the owner was at least three miles away. The funny thing was that not only is this seemingly quite common, but the dog cannot be tricked because when they had a stranger drive the owners car into the driveway, the dog would not respond at all. So their response wasn't dependent on the sound of the car or the regular schedule kept by the owner. It seemed that just the decision/intention by the owner to go home was the only cue necessary for the dog to prepare itself for his imminent arrival by somehow naturally tuning in to the consciousness that pervades our universe.

For me, this confirmed what the scientists and saints say

(actions in life) have already happened, and we are not the doer of actions as we have been led to believe. But rather, are witnessing life unfolding as it will. At the absolute level we can commit no sin because we commit no action. We don't willfully do any action, so how can we commit a sin? In this way we are absolved from Sin and Guilt.

However, try and tell us this liberating information on one of those guilty days when we feel trapped by the illusion, and believe everything to be real and we the victims of our circumstance, adrift on an ocean of uncertainty. In this state of disconnect, it's like trying to put a cord into the wrong electrical outlet. We have to be vigilant everyday with our minds, because the unconscious guilt projects onto everything in our world, and makes us believe we are hated, unworthy, guilty and so we need help.

This undertaking requires the assistance of a higher power, whether that is in the form of Jesus, Buddha, Muhammad, a guru, Source, Universe, or grace from God directly. The esoteric aspect of various paths and religions generally delve more deeply into healing the core separation. This is the outlet we need to plug into in order to help dissolve this illusion that we have believed to be real.

Many things arise in our life that are challenging and they bring up our feelings of guilt and fear.

- This guilt arises when we are financially stressed, we become scared or feel bad, or we think, "*What's wrong with me, I can't keep up?*" And so we get angry and then project our fear and guilt onto others.
- When we are unwell and helpless, we feel guilty for being a burden on others because we can't be as productive as others, hence we compare ourselves and this leads to our projecting more guilt onto our body because of our judgments. This only serves to make us feel even more

unwell and small.

- Even when we are dying, there is a guilt that we are incomplete somehow and not worthy enough to meet our maker.
- Or a mother never feels like she succeeded and so constantly experiences guilt and projects it outwardly, usually at someone in her family.

All of these situations take us back to the pain of our original separation, because we deeply believe our obstacles and our toxic thoughts are real. Notice how there is a trap in each situation that keeps the fear/guilt cycling. For instance, "*I'm **not** good enough, I'll **never** succeed; I'm **not worthy** enough; God will **reject** me; I'm **flawed** because I am sick; **God does not love me**; I am **poor** and God has **left** me because something is **wrong with me.**"

This is where we need to become the warrior and use the sword of discrimination to say "NO! This is a lie." Use the energy of the inner anger, and transform it into its evolved form – the energy of Power. With your imaginary sword slice through the regret and affirm, "*I am already one with the Divine/God ... I no longer believe that I am wrong and deserve to suffer ... This must stop now! I am immortal spirit, not a limited body ... My strength comes from my Spirit – not from anything of the world ... I am innocent, loved and fearless ... please (insert Deity of your choice)_____ enter into me and replace the ego/mind with the mind of pure spirit.*"

If by chance, you don't have immediate access to an imaginary warrior's sword, there is a very powerful kinesthetic exercise that you can do, anywhere and anytime, to take you from the ego mind to the mind of wholeness or Oneness. A Swami I know said that the index finger represents the Ego. He also said, that when we join the index finger with the thumb (representing the universal self), we are containing the energy – as in meditation, (also known as Chin Mudra).

So if you find yourself affected by the unconscious guilt, where you are out of control, maybe angry, frightened or overwhelmed, or anything at all that has pulled you away from your center or peacefulness, then simply join your thumb and index fingers, thereby making a perfect "O" and silently say to yourself, "*I am not a victim, I am whole and innocent.*" Then feel a wave of calm and peace wash over you and allow it to cleanse all of your false identifications that have been wrongly telling you that you are less than perfect. Do this as often as you feel drawn to and let it become a habit; this will cleanse us every time we think poorly of ourselves or of another, as this gesture symbolizes the merging of the individual soul with the universal soul.

At the very least, when the old programs rear their ugly heads, see them all as simply, "Data" and say, "Thank you" and "I love you." Remembering that they don't define you nor are they you.

It is only with the help of a higher power or inner Spirit that any significant transformation can occur, because on our own we are limited to the boundaries of the lower mind, but in order to go beyond it, we need Grace.

Original Sin/Guilt is simply missing the mark and putting the plug into the wrong socket. The wrong socket creates dissonance and great upset. It animates illusion to the point where we believe every word it tells us. This is where we fall into the snares of the Snake of Satan or the belief in Original Sin.

Even though, the illusion seems all-powerful, (this in itself is an illusion), it has no true power on its own other than what we give to it. Knowing this, then one solution is that we can simply pull the plug from the world and re-connect to the true source of power, which dissolves all concepts, all dualities, in fact, this very world. When there's no longer a world, there can be no sin, no guilt, no origin, no Original anything.

All that's left is the Absolute Love prior to consciousness itself. Love is the medicine that puts to death all of our unconscious guilt and fear.

"Love says 'I am everything' Wisdom says "I am nothing' between the two my life flows."
Nisargadatta Maharaj

4.9 SURRENDER

*"I've been abandoned, God has forgotten all about me because I'm
not thinking positively enough, my intentions aren't clear enough
and I'm not making enough money. Why would God have anything
to do with someone as unsuccessful as me?"*

These are common refrains I've heard over and over again. The
Internet has seemingly replaced God and we've transferred our
guilt from religion to, "I did something wrong!" because we're
not living up to a New Age paradigm that says we are supposed
to be: dynamic, grounded, present, positive, have a clear intent,
sexy, rich and abundantly happy not to mention being
"awakened."

Our relentless search for truth ultimately confuses us, because
we question the value of our innocence and we doubt ourselves.
I remember going through a period in my life where I was very
un-grounded and spacey in fact – I was never where I was
supposed to be. I judged myself harshly for not being, "In my
body," which was the New Age catch phrase of the time.

I was living in an ashram at the time, so I decided to approach
the Guru – and ask her why I was not in my body. Her answer to
my question, something you would never find on the Internet
was, *"It's none of your business."* Immediately I felt as though a
burden had lifted from my shoulders, I had been relieved of
Guilt Duty. I felt that her words, *"It's none of your business,"* gave
me permission to simply, "Be," thereby allowing all of my self-
judgments to fall away. The grip of guilt had been released. My
body, which had previously been filled with doubt, guilt and
judgment, was overflowing with light and peace.

I realized that as long as we struggle to create or do or change,
we are struggling against, and resisting the inspired, Divine
truth that is trying to shape our life. If we could only be still and

open long enough to receive it and act on its inspiration rather than acting from our mind, fear and busyness, then true peace would be ours. There are so many factors beyond the little personality/ego that we aren't even aware of. We are part of a great puzzle that has been designed by the Creator who knows the big picture, because 'life' has already been scripted. A flower can blossom with a beautiful scent, but no matter how great a gardener we are, we have no control over its blossoming. The blossoming is not our responsibility nor is it any of our business.

In the meantime, there is nothing wrong with thinking positive thoughts, holding an intention or focusing on being successful or creative. It ultimately doesn't matter because when it is our time to live a different life or awaken to the truth, we will. This might be why many teachings exhort us to do our actions to the best of our ability, just not to be attached to the results, "fruits." In a teaching video, Dr. Hew Len said, *"holding an intention is nothing more than a clear premonition."* It couldn't be any other way because what is ours will come to us, besides, it's already happened and so you cannot manifest something that is not already yours.

In a video, I saw many years ago, Living, Loving and Aids, Dr. Elisabeth Kubler-Ross spoke about surrender. She realized that saying the words, *"Not my will but thy will Lord,"* in her prayers was not sufficient, and it was only after many years that she discovered the need for one more line to be added. *"Not my time, but thy time Lord."* When we think that we should be somewhere, or doing something and even try to bend time to make these things happen, this is a common trap. It causes such stress and guilt not only in the efforting and the striving but also in the self-judgments that are sure to follow should we not reach our goals within the timeframes we set. Dr. Ross's example demonstrates the maturity and the wisdom that is gleaned from many years of experience. Complete surrendering of Will and Time.

When we step out of our Source, we will immediately feel

guilt because we have placed our attention on the illusion, i.e. ideas and concepts, rather than on what we really are, pure Divinity. Thus, when we feel guilt or doubt, we can use it as a sign or a reminder to return to the surrender – to the state of peaceful oneness, remembering that we are in the arms of our Beloved and that it is, "None of our business," why we are where we are. All of our good ideas and dreams and intentions are useless if they are not aligned with what the Divine has scripted. There is a great line that says, "*If you want to make God laugh, tell Him your plans.*" We don't truly know what we need to be experiencing in our lives – or when – and it may not look anything like what others seem to be experiencing but is perfect for you.

All guilt stems from the belief that we've separated from Source. When we remember that this is the lie, then we can guilt-lessly return to and bathe in the real source of all love, all life and all truth. Surrender is emptying ourselves of the misconceptions and the lies because when our cup has been filled with fallacies, there is no room for the Divine to pour in the real Nectar, which heals everything. So empty your cup of blame, return to your innocence and drink from the waters of eternal life.

In therapy you are responsible for your deeds. In spirituality,
all deeds are God's deeds.
Student of Ramesh Balsekar

4.10 QUANTUM LOVE

In the biblical parable known as "The Prodigal Son," the younger of two sons, asks his father to give him his share of the estate. After receiving his money, this son heads out to travel to distant lands and squanders his new found wealth on prostitutes and parties. Then a famine hits the land and the son, now penniless, is forced to work at a pig farm. He laments working in such wretched conditions for poor wages. He envies the pigs as they seem to be fed better food than he. The son reflects on his father's farm. His father treated his workers with respect, decent food and paid them fairly. The son decides that he would return home and seek work as a farm hand. He plans to announce to his father upon seeing him, *'Father, I have sinned against heaven ... I am not worthy to be called your son ... Make me as one of your hired servants.'*

He returned to his father, but while he was still at a distance, his father saw him, and ran towards him, and kissed him. The father gave the son a robe and put a ring on his finger and called for a celebratory feast. But the older son, upon hearing of the return complains to his father, *"Why are you embracing him after he has betrayed you and become lost?"* His father responds *"But it was appropriate to celebrate and be glad, for this, your brother, was dead, and is alive again. He was lost, and is found."* (43)

Why this story is powerful, is because it is our story. We've all strayed and become lost in our worldly journey. We've become caught in some way and left to feel like an undeserving "sinner" and believe unconsciously that we need to be punished by a "vengeful and condemning" God for our perceived mistakes. However, the surprise ending is that just as the father in the story embraces his son with open arms upon his return home, we too are embraced and fully "forgiven" for our wrong understandings.

John Newton had written the words to the familiar hymn,

Amazing Grace. This hymn exemplifies this situation beautifully. *"... I once was lost but now am found,"* and, *"Was blind but now I see."*

- We've been lost believing this world is real rather than a dream.
- We've walked around lost and deeply upset for all of the wrong reasons.
- We've been lost by believing that we are separate from and unloved by God.
- We've been lost by feeling guilty all of the time – but not knowing it – and instead we blamed and projected unconscious guilt onto ourselves and others and hence caused suffering.
- We've also been lost trying to find our home, where we really belong and where we will be welcomed like the prodigal son once we've realized that this place that we wander in can never satisfy us.
- We have been lost living in our ego-mind; and unless we leap free of that conditioning, we will be lost forever thus keeping the nightmare alive.

"Was blind ..."

- We've been blind to the beauty of the Divine within.
- We've been blind to the Divine beauty in everyone we meet.
- We've been blind to the God that lives in every single thing that we can perceive or conceive.
- We've been blind as we have searched and searched for love in all the wrong places.
- We've been blind because we've been wearing the wrong prescription called ego and guilt and so everything that we saw looked dark and unclear.

- We've also been blinded and tricked by outer appearances, and we have defined others and ourselves as limited, physical beings that sin and are guilty.

"But now I see …"

As with the prodigal son, the grace has never left us nor have we abandoned it. For we are It, we are carried on it, and this grace, this love, lives within you as you. And just as the nightmare of guilt hides deep within us, so too does the solution, but the solution is true and real, innocent and pure and it has never judged us or held us in the darkness of guilt.

This love, this grace waits patiently for us to return to our true home. Our blindness shall be removed, and we shall see that all this was really just a dream. We will finally "See" that we have always been deeply loved beyond anything of the world. Our sins are forgiven and seen as mere shadows in a dream. Our Quantum Guilt turns to Quantum Love, which is a metaphysical love, an infinite love, it's the consciousness that we all share. Quantum love surpasses all worldly love and erases the perception of guilt and sin and elevates our whole world to a higher frequency allowing us to make a quantum leap to freedom and release our belief in guilt and sin thereby returning us to perfect peace.

Om purnamadah purnamidam purnat purnamudacyate,
Purnasya purnamadaya purnamevavsisyate.
Peace Invocation from the Yajur Veda

Translation:
Om. That is perfect. This is perfect.
From the perfect springs the perfect. If the perfect is taken from the perfect, the perfect remains.

EPILOGUE

WHY WE ARE NOT GUILTY

1/ Our main reason for guilt and suffering is that we believe we've separated from our source. But in fact, we've never left our source and remain one with it. So we are not guilty.

2/ This world is an illusion and so are we. An illusion or echo has no power to separate from its source. Quantum physicist, David Bohm, states that the universe itself is a projection or hologram. Nisargadatta Maharaj, an East Indian Mystic has said, "There is no birth, there is no death, it's all an illusion." So everything we experience is a dream and there is no guilt in a dream.

3/ What we think we are experiencing now is actually a dream and there is no real entity that can be guilty.

4/ All of life in this dream is scripted. All physical laws and the fate of every molecule is predetermined and has already happened. Science now agrees with this theory. Everything that is to occur has already been set in motion. You are not the doer of actions but rather an actor reading lines already written. When you experience déjà vu, you are getting a taste of something that has already occurred. So if there is no doer of actions, who is guilty?

5/ In a dream, the actor (just like in the movies) is always searching to find their way out of fear, difficulty and unconscious guilt. The characters attack each other because they feel guilty about themselves. They project this guilt outward in the hopes of getting some relief. But the actors don't know that everyone and everything in a dream is of the same substance, so there is nothing really to struggle against.

6/ The time spent in this movie–dream would be much easier if the actors knew that they were all of the same substance. Just as H^2O remains the same whether it is in the form of fluid, ice or steam, so too the actors are all one substance and remain with their divine source, regardless of how they are portrayed. But in their delusion, they see only separation and disappointment. Because each being is a part of Source, and Source is love, the actors unfortunately search for love in all of the wrong places not understanding that the love they seek is already within them. This misguided searching often leads to addiction, depression, guilt and anger. This is why enlightened beings come to help us. They are free from the dream, and can help guide us from violence, guilt and fear, to have respect for others and all of life.

7/ When one awakens from the dream, one realizes there is no separation. Great compassion then arises and we see all that exists as innocent and guiltless. We see everything with divine eyes and understand that we are loved beyond anything that the physical body/mind could even begin to comprehend.

8/ Saying "I Love You" to all that you encounter will put to death all guilt and illusion in your world.

BIBLIOGRAPHY

1/ Renard, Gary. *The Disappearance of the Universe*. Hay House, 2008. (p. 325)

2/ Talbot, Michael.
http://www.mail-archive.com/mythfolk@yahoogroups
.com/msg00444.html, (p. 1)

3/ Talbot, Michael.
http://www.mail-archive.com/mythfolk@yahoogroups
.com/msg00444.html, (p. 3)

4/ Norretranders, Tor. *The User Illusion*. Penguin Group, 1999. (p. 345)

5/ *A Course in Miracles*, Foundation for Inner Peace, 2007. (p. x)

6/ "Taken from – www.allaboutscience.org/big-bang-theory.htm – published by AllAboutGOD.com Ministries, M. Houdmann, P. Matthews-Rose, R. Niles, editors, 2002-2012. Used by permission."

7/ Wapnick, Ken PhD, from online: *Foundation for a Course in Miracles: The Metaphysics of Separation and Forgiveness*. http://www.facim.org/excerpts/s3e3.htm

8/ *A Course in Miracles*, Foundation for Inner Peace, 2007. ACIM Text 13, 1:1-2

9/ Singh, Kirpal. *The Wheel of Life*. Ruhani Satsang-Divine Science of the Soul, 2000. (p. 38)

10/ Wapnick, Ken PhD, from online: *Foundation for a Course in Miracles*: http://www.facim.org/excerpts/s11e7.htm, p.2

11/ Talbot, Michael, *The Holographic Universe*. Harper Collins Publishers, 1992. (p. 40)

12/ Wolinsky, Stephen. *The Nirvana Sutras and Advaita-Vedanta*. Quantum Institute, 2005. (p. 175)

13/ *A Course in Miracles*. Foundation for Inner Peace, 2007, ACIM T-13.II.1-3

14/ Talbot, Michael.
http://www.mail-archive.com/mythfolk@yahoogroups.com /msg00444.html, p. 2

15/ Singh, Rajinder. *Empowering Your Soul Through Meditation*. Element, 1999. (p.98)

16/ *A Course in Miracles*, Foundation for Inner Peace, 2007, ACIM T-13.I.3:2-4

17/ Bagga, Raj Kumar. *Ocean of Love, The Anurag Sagar of Kabir*. Sant Bani Ashram, 1995. (p. xxvii)

18/ Parsons, Tony. *As It Is*. Inner Directions, 2004. (p. 62)

19/ Wolinsky, Stephen Ph.D. *Beginner's Guide to Quantum Psychology*. Bramble Books, 2000. (p. 23)

20/ Muktananda, Swami. *Who Am I?* / *Darshan Magazine*. Syda Foundation, 1999. (p.35)

21/ Bohm, David. (from: Michael Talbot), *The Holographic*

Universe. Harper Collins Publishers, 1992. (p. 48)

22/ Singh, Kirpal. *The Crown of Life.* Sawan Kirpal Publications, 1985. (p. 136)

23/ Singh, Kirpal. *The Crown of Life.* Sawan Kirpal Publications. 1985. (p. 137)

24/ Talbot, Michael. http://www.mail-archive.com/mythfolk@yahoogroups.com /msg00444.html, p. 2

25/ Maharshi, Ramana. *Letters From Sri Ramanasramam.* V.S. Ramanan-Sri Ramanasramam, 2006. (p.36)

26/ Wolinsky, Stephen Ph. D. *You Are Not – Beyond the Three Veils of Consciousness.* Quantum Institute Press, 2002. (p. 28)

27/ *A Course in Miracles.* Foundation for Inner Peace, 2007, ACIM – Manual for Teachers, p. 36

28/ *A Course in Miracles.* Foundation for Inner Peace, 2007, ACIM T-29.VI.2:14 p. 616

29/ Renard, Gary. *The Disappearance of the Universe.* Hay House, Inc., 2008. (p. 330)

30/ Balsekar, Ramesh. *Who Cares?!* Advaita Press, 1999. (p. 62)

31/ Maharaj, Nisargadatta. *The Wisdom-Teachings of Nisargadatta Maharaj.* Inner Directions Publishing, 2003. (p. 121)

32/ Wolinsky, Stephen. *The Nirvana Sutras and Advaita-Vedanta.* Quantum Institute, 2005, Sutra xvii. (p. 58)

33/ Wolinsky, Stephen. *The Nirvana Sutras and Advaita-Vedanta.* Quantum Institute, 2005, Sutra iv. (p. 31)

34/ Shafer, Dr. Aaron. http://www.thetech.org/exhibits/online/ ugenetics/ask.php?id=166

35/ Pursah – from Renard, Gary. *The Disappearance of the Universe.* Hay House, Inc. 2008. (p. 328)

36/ Singh, Rajinder. *Silken Thread of the Divine.* SK Publications, 2005. (p. 18)

37/ Posted by Jordon, Rumor Mill News. http://www.rumormillnews.com/cgi-bin/archive.cgi?read =239664

38/ Rinpoche, Sakyong Mipham. http://radiofreeshambhala.org /index.php?s=when+you%27re+happy

39/ Rohr, Richard. *Everything Belongs.* Crossroad Publishing Company, 2003. (p 60)

40/ Laval, Devrah. *The Magic Doorway into the Divine.* Mystic Lights Publishing, 2007. (p. 346)

41/ McCraty, Roland Ph.D., *The Electrophysiology of Intuition*, From the DVD – *The Living Matrix.* Becker Massey LLC. 2009

42/ Sheldrake, Rupert. Cited by: Manjir Samanta-Laughton, MD., *Punk Science.* O-Books, 2006. (p. 84)

43/ Prodigal Son Paraphrased from – Luke 15:32, *King James Version.* Random House, 1991

About the Author

Devrah Laval is the author of *The Magic Doorway into the Divine*, an international bestseller on Amazon.

At the age of twenty-nine, Devrah Laval – master counselor, facilitator, and author had a life-altering mystical experience along with a profound physical healing that awakened her to her own true nature.

Since that time, Devrah has facilitated groups and individuals to help them more fully realize the potential of their own radiant Self.

Devrah's website is: www.devrahlaval.com

To receive information on upcoming workshops, speaking engagements future articles or news, please sign-up for her newsletter or write to: info@devrahlaval.com

BOOKS

O is a symbol of the world, of oneness and unity. In different cultures it also means the "eye," symbolizing knowledge and insight. We aim to publish books that are accessible, constructive and that challenge accepted opinion, both that of academia and the "moral majority."

Our books are available in all good English language bookstores worldwide. If you don't see the book on the shelves ask the bookstore to order it for you, quoting the ISBN number and title. Alternatively you can order online (all major online retail sites carry our titles) or contact the distributor in the relevant country, listed on the copyright page.

See our website **www.o-books.net** for a full list of over 500 titles, growing by 100 a year.

And tune in to myspiritradio.com for our book review radio show, hosted by June-Elleni Laine, where you can listen to the authors discussing their books.